THE PHILOSOPHER'S DESIRE

Psychoanalysis, Interpretation, and Truth

D1616951

William Egginton

STANFORD UNIVERSITY PRESS

STANFORD, CALIFORNIA

2007

Stanford University Press
Stanford, California

Printed in the United States of America on acid-free, archival-quality paper

Library of Congress Cataloging-in-Publication Data

Egginton, William, 1969–
    The philosopher's desire : psychoanalysis, interpretation, and truth /
William Egginton.
        p.   cm.
    Includes bibliographical references and index.
    ISBN 978-0-8047-5599-3 (cloth : alk. paper)
    ISBN 978-0-8047-5600-6 (pbk. : alk. paper)
    1. Psychoanalysis and philosophy.   2. Hermeneutics.   I. Title.
BF175.4.P45E44 2007
150.19'5—dc22   2007001245

Typeset by Westchester Book Group in 11/13.5 Garamond

THE PHILOSOPHER'S DESIRE

Contents

Acknowledgments

Thanks are due to Aimee Woznick, my research assistant, who edited this piece when it was at its roughest; to all the students in my seminar on Freud and interpretation at the University at Buffalo, and to Joan Copjec, who asked me to teach it; to the students in my course on Lacan, Deleuze, and Derrida at the University of St. Petersburg, Russia, to John Bailyn, who organized that summer, and to James McFarland, who substituted for me numerous times during my daughter's illness; to Chris Celenza, for his learned consultations and help with translating Pliny; to my friends and colleagues in the Philosophical Reading Group at UB, and especially to David E. Johnson and Martin Hägglund, who have helped enormously in my thinking about the issues in this book; to Gregg Lambert, who read the manuscript so carefully and knew just what it needed; to Kevin Heller, whose sharp eyes and keen wit were at work on previous books as well; to Lisa Block de Behar, Biagio D'Angelo, and the organizers of the ICLA meeting in Lima, Peru, where a chapter of this book was presented; to Koji Kawamoto, Takagi Shigemitsu, Tadashi Uchino, and Ohsawa Yoshihiro (in memoriam), who generously invited me to present some of this work in Japan; to Leah Middlebrook and David Castillo, for the opportunity to present a chapter as part of the "Subjects and Objects" speaker series at the University of Oregon; to Maureen Jameson, Martha Malamud, Charles Stinger, and Uday Sukhatme for their support in providing me a year's sabbatical to work on this and other projects; to Norris Pope and Emily Jane Cohen at Stanford University Press, as well as Rebecca Homiski and Ellen Lohman, for their excellent work in editing and producing the book; and above all to my wife, Bernadette Wegenstein, for her constant presence in my life, intellectual and emotional, and to my children, Alexander and Charlotte, for helping me see the world for the first time again. This book is dedicated to them.

THE PHILOSOPHER'S DESIRE

Prologue: Interpretive Strings

The twentieth century, which began with the invention of one of the most powerful interpretive models the world had ever seen, psychoanalysis, saw at least two more follow, the philosophical hermeneutics of Heidegger and Gadamer, and structuralism, before witnessing a series of intellectual movements united by their suspicion toward interpretation in all its stripes.[1] In the world of literary and cultural studies today, hermeneutics and structuralism could seem to be merely momentary whims in an intellectual history moving inexorably toward the atrophy of all strong models of interpretation, toward what Vattimo and Rovatti memorably called a *pensiero debole*.[2] Alone among such models, psychoanalysis persists, but seemingly in a state of constant antagonism besieged by cultural conservatives who have always found its theories laughably lacking in scientific rationale and cultural radicals who accuse it of inflicting violence on its objects of analysis through the imposition of its own culturally and historically specific fantasies.

The Philosopher's Desire is in large part an argument against this picture. On the one hand, psychoanalysis has never been a strong model of interpretation, if what one means by that is a model that replaces the object of its analysis with a meaning purported to be lying beyond or inside it, just outside view for the uninitiated. On the other hand, the posthermeneutic and poststructuralist discourses that have claimed to be rid of interpretation have in fact never lost sight of it, or at least have never been free of a kind of interpretation that psychoanalysis and twentieth-century hermeneutics largely discovered.

There are many protagonists in this story and many ways to tell it. The path I have chosen to trace is largely concerned with the innovations bequeathed to the psychoanalytic theory of interpretation by Jacques Lacan, while the way I have chosen to tell it has been suggested by interpretation itself. Each of the four chapters of this book is organized around what I am calling an interpretive string. A string is like a series in that it is sequential, but unlike a series a string assumes a connection. A string ties together what comes before with what comes after, and strings may themselves be tied to other strings. In the strings that form each of the book's sections, a concept, problem, or text is followed through a particular interpretive string it has endured. It is my hope that by the end of the book what appeared at the outset to be four separate strings will be revealed as in fact a single string, a labyrinth of the kind Borges once described as consisting of a single line. In the first string, the concept of interpretation itself is at stake, and it is followed through Sigmund Freud's seminal work on interpretation, *The Interpretation of Dreams.* The second string begins with a particular text, Daniel Paul Schreber's memoir of his experience with psychosis, and follows this text respectively through its interpretation by Freud, the interpretation of Freud's text by Lacan, and the interpretation of that text in turn by Gilles Deleuze and Félix Guattari. The third string is initiated by the seminar Lacan chose to spearhead the 1966 publication of his *Écrits*: his reading of Edgar Allan Poe's "The Purloined Letter." This reading famously sparked a debate with Jacques Derrida, who used his own counterinterpretation of Poe's story as a pivot for deconstructing what he viewed as Lacan's pretensions to an exclusive orientation toward truth. This debate leads finally to the fourth string, which ties together a series of philosophical and literary interventions on the concept of time. While Derrida debates Heidegger's notion of two kinds of temporality as vigorously as he chides Lacan for his pretensions to truth, I use that chapter to argue that the three discourses are largely in agreement and that what separates them is in fact a misunderstanding about the role and nature of interpretation.

What do we mean when we speak of interpretation? In the opening string I discuss what could be a deconstructive and posthermeneutic understanding of the term and then try to show how precisely such an understanding can be seen to emerge from Freud's early work on dream interpretation. If classical interpretive models can be called monologic in that they assume a unidirectional relation between a surface text to be read and an underlying meaning to be revealed, psychoanalysis, along with the hermeneutic practice inspired by Heidegger, suggests that the psychoanalytic subject or Dasein be understood as a bipolar logos, a shuttling back and forth between terms that produces meaning in its movement rather than finding meaning already there.

In light of such a picture of the subject, the moment of interpretation—for example, of a dream—appears in Freud's study as a moment of dynamic creation rather than passive discovery. What I call "the awakening" delineates the problematic relation between thought and experience, inserting an operative space into sensual experience that both de-liberates it from thought and temporalizes it, allowing it *to have been* experienced. While the awakening is necessary for rational thought and communication, it also retroactively closes or decides a series of often mutually exclusive possibilities, collapsing a suspended series into a concrete string. This string can always be seen as the effect of a series of exclusions of lost possibilities, which themselves remain inscribed in the unconscious in the form of what I have called the fault-line, forming the basis for our fundamental ethical orientation and our most deeply seated desires.

One immediate result of the ideas emerging from the interpretation string is that we must distinguish between at least two levels of interpretation, one primary and one secondary. This distinction becomes central to the psychosis string. Primary interpretation is the active, productive shuttling internal to the subject as a bipolar logos, the transformations of words that are productive of meaning. Secondary interpretation is modeled on the awakening, a moment of retroactive decision that collapses a vibrant series of possible meanings into a past experience or thought. The problem, however, is that although primary interpretation would seem to be a force restrained, trapped, by its belated sibling, in fact there can be no liberation of the primary. Secondary interpretation is the de-liberation of the primary that allows it to have been, and a failure of secondary interpretation leads not to liberation but to psychosis, an absolute alienation in an incommunicable world. It is at this juncture that Deleuze and Guattari enter with their famous critique of psychoanalysis and its Oedipus complex. *Anti-Oedipus* and its sequel, *A Thousand Plateaus*, have long been interpreted as battle cries against psychoanalysis's stifling of primary interpretation's productive desire by the imposition of a phallocentric, normatively obsessed paternal function. Another version of secondary interpretation, however, must be at work in Deleuze and Guattari's thought, one that ensures that despite some disputed terminology their project and Lacan's are largely in harmony.

The third, or purloined, string also has a debate in French letters at its core, albeit the letter in question was originally an American one. Derrida's critique of Lacan as "The Purveyor of Truth" has sparked its own international debate; however, beyond agreeing with those who have found flaws in Derrida's interpretation of Lacan, what I seek to expose is how Lacan's seminar functions as well as any other Lacanian text to do exactly what Derrida later praised Lacan for in what could be considered his personal eulogy. In that text, "For the Love of Lacan," Derrida said that Lacan knew perhaps better than anyone else how to read "the singular desire of the philosopher,"[3] and it is my contention that the "Seminar on the Purloined Letter" is the epitome of this reading. Whereas Derrida interprets the seminar as proposing that all communicative acts are anchored by a fundamental reference to a lost but coveted origin, for me the seminar is a parable of philosophy, specifically of the philosopher's desire, which always leads him or her to search for symbolic truths in imaginary places. Lacan, then, is offering an intervention, in the language of psychoanalysis, in the field of philosophy. It is an intervention around the problem of truth and the desire of philosophy in relation to that truth, and the theory of that relation is the theory of interpretation.

These three strings together lead inexorably to what is perhaps the most profound and inevitable of all problems, that of time, in that the very possibility of experience, interpretation, and truth is inconceivable without reference to temporal change. In the temporality string I explore what the Derridean and Lacanian notions of *spacing* have to say about time and its relation to interpretation. In the course of this discussion, the debate staged between Derrida and Lacan on the issue of truth is overlaid on a similar debate between Derrida and the thought of Martin Heidegger on the notion of time. The literature of several modern Latin American writers—Borges, García Márquez, Roa Bastos—becomes the basis for an exploration of the fictional and impossible notion of a completely saturated experience of the world. Such an experience, it turns out, could be no experience at all.

Whether in the shape of a town beset by absolute forgetting or a man endowed with absolute memory, the saturation of life with no recourse to abstraction, minimal distance, or generality leads to a kind of negation of life as experience. What is required for experience to be possible, as well as for either memory or forgetting to be possible, is the minimal distance of signification, or spacing.

Spacing, which Derrida also describes as the work of *differance*, is on the one hand equivalent to secondary interpretation and on the other hand responsible for the production of time as a series of nows, or what Heidegger called vulgar time. The distinction, however, between a vulgar time that Dasein "falls into" and a primordial or "original" time is the target of Derrida's critique. Despite this conflict, what this string demonstrates through an extended interpretation of Jorge Luis Borges's story "Funes the Memorious" is that Lacan, Heidegger, *and* Derrida ultimately have similar notions of something akin to the spacing at the heart of temporality. Where Lacan and Heidegger would seem to agree and Derrida to disagree is on the issue of how one talks about time—on the role, in other words, of interpretation. Whereas Derrida takes issue with the famous distinction between an authentic and an inauthentic mode of being—essentially the same bone he has to pick with Lacan's way of talking about truth—both Heidegger and Lacan seem to acknowledge the danger of an illusion at the heart of much philosophical thought and the distinction between reproducing that illusion and revealing it as illusion.

This illusion, which is referred to in the title *The Philosopher's Desire*, is that the possibility of a pure repetition promised by the signifier can in fact be redeemed in reality, in the imaginary register. Inauthentic thinking, in this view, is a thinking founded on that illusion. Although none of the discourses analyzed accepts the premise of that illusion, in his critiques of Lacan and Heidegger Derrida accuses the discourses that make that distinction of themselves falling prey to the illusion. By distinguishing between on the one hand an inauthentic philosophical discourse that locates truth in an impossible imaginary repetition or a direct, monologic reference of the word to its corresponding thing and on the other hand an authentic philosophical discourse that exposes the impossibility of such reference, that insists on the production of meaning at the heart of a bipolar logos, the philosopher in Derrida's view has necessarily placed his bets on the former and hailed himself as a purveyor or truth. Yet the truth thus purveyed is of an entirely different nature. It is a duplicitous truth that recognizes its own duplicity, that speaks in the language of truth in order to show that truth is something other than what it has been understood to be. Those interpreters who understand the object of interpretation to be itself not an object in the world, an imaginary answer to a symbolic question, but rather the constantly renewed product of an interpretation already at work making the world—those interpreters have read the philosopher's singular desire and seen in it their own.

1

The Interpretation String

The first string is a string about strings, about how interpretation as the bone of contention of so much of contemporary critical theory is at the same time the tie that binds its disparate strands together. Therefore, while we will broach in this chapter discourses as varied as Kierkegaard's ruminations on Abraham's sacrifice and Heidegger's exposition of Dasein as the being for whom its own being is a question, the centerpiece will be Freud's *Interpretation of Dreams*. This text, whose creation serendipitously opens the twentieth century and shares a birth year with Jacques Lacan, became as much the touchstone for a new hermeneutical practice as the target of its vituperation and catalyst of its downfall. At stake will be the question of the extent to which the interpretive strategies described by Freud might—rather than prescribing a closed, constraining reading practice bent on replacing the richness of individual experience with the cold triumvirate of the Oedipal triangle—in fact have taken some of the first steps toward a critical philosophical perspective largely associated today with poststructuralism.

The Bipolar Logos

What is at stake when we speak of interpretation? If we begin from the perspective of deconstruction, a method that nonetheless shuns identification as an interpretive practice in any traditional sense of the word, one technique we might employ to interpret the word *interpretation* would be to approach the word etymologically, practicing what Deleuze and Guattari[1] have called "a distinctly philosophical form of acrobatics" in search of Heidegger's original word, "the word, as it once was when it was word."[2] As Borges writes, "[t]here are few disciplines as interesting as etymology; this is due to the unpredictable transformations of the primitive meaning of words across time. Given such transformations, which can border on the paradoxical, the origin of a word will help little or not at all in the clarification of a concept."[3]

Now, if word origin helps little or not at all in the clarification of a concept, then what possibly could be the purpose in practicing the discipline of etymology, in tracing those unpredictable transformations across time that border on the paradoxical? If the purpose is not the clarification of concepts, then it must be that something else—namely, the unpredictable transformations of primitive meaning—is the source of his interest. If transformations are unpredictable, they occur without being pre-dicted, without being said before they occur; or, they occur in the saying, and it is the saying and only the saying that produces them. Indeed, a predictable transformation would be nothing short of oxymoronic, given that a word fore-said, prior to its transformation, were it the same word as that said after its transformation, would have undergone neither the transition nor the formation implicit in said transformation.

This foray into etymology is not gratuitous, for in deconstructive practice reading entails the release of a certain transformative mobility in words and a refusal to grant them the social and historical stability demanded by notions of primitive or original meaning on the one hand, or mere pragmatics on the other. For the former, the word or phrase can only mean what tradition claimed for it; for the latter, it is reduced to its use in a given community or social context. A deconstructive reading, however, is one that seeks the release of a word from such bondage and draws its strength from a kind of shuttling back and forth between the two. Indeed, what deconstructive reading reveals is that the so-called meaning of the word cannot be stabilized in either tradition or use-context, quite simply because that meaning does not underlie secondary or parasitical transformations but is rather itself the product or effect of those transformations.[4]

Meaning is, of course, what is sought in interpretation, and deconstruction's apparent antipathy to interpretation could easily stem from the

notion that interpretation seeks meaning under or beyond its transformations.[5] Yet perhaps this notion is erroneous; perhaps another interpretation
would release interpretation from this pragmatic/traditionalist bondage.
Meaning, *Bedeutung* in German, is the solidification of a process, *Deutung*
("interpretation"). *Deuten*, to interpret, comes from the old high German
for *Volk*, or people—hence its assonance with *Deutch*—and its original
sense would have been something like "to translate into the common language or the language of the people." To interpret is to put it into plain
words, as it were, words unencumbered by the need for translation, words
in use, pragmatic words. For what needs interpretation if not something
spoken in another tongue, words, a statement perhaps, but also a state in
need of translation? Indeed, parallel etymology would corroborate this with
another early equivalent, *Übersetzung*, "translation."[6]

In our Latinate languages, to interpret is formed of *inter*, between,
and the Sanskrit *prath*, meaning to spread out, as in to spread the wealth as
one does in French should one be involved in the action *prêter*, to borrow
or to lend depending on one's syntactic position. The phrase "Neither a
borrower nor a lender be" might be sound economic sense in Polonius's
world of advice-giving, but in the world of sense-making it will surely take
the wind from our sails because it is only by borrowing and lending, by
transferring our words, that the words take on the kind of exchange value
we call meaning. When Polonius asks him what he reads, Hamlet responds,
"Words, words, words." Pressed as to what the "matter" of those words
might be, Hamlet replies, "Between who?" capturing in the "inappropri-
ateness" of his answer-question the interminable flight of the very meaning, or matter, Polonius seeks—insofar as what he seeks is stable matter,
and not the fugitive borrowing-and-lending between communicative or
interpretive poles that constitutes the real matter of meaning.[7]

Jean-Luc Nancy[8] speaks of the sense of the world because sense, *sens*
in French, conveys not only meaning but also direction, motion, and hence
what he (with others) calls the *spacing* required to be toward something or
someone. Moreover, *sens*, or *sentido* as "meaning" doubles up in French or
Spanish for a redundancy that might be expressed in English in the sentence, "In what sense do you mean?" English speakers enjoy the security
that in whatever sense a word might be taken or meant it still has a meaning despite or independent of such misappropriations. Yet the meaning,
the *Bedeutung* in German, is also only ever a *Meinung*, as Hegel notes,[9]

and hence only ever *mein*, which is to say: my take, my appropriation, is written into the word itself, its history, or its traces. So whether we speak of its sense or its meaning, what is retained is the movement of an appropriation, a shuttling, a directionality, and a borrowing and lending. This is another way of saying that there is no meaning independent of a word's appropriation or misappropriation in sense, independent of its transformation between poles, independent of its interpretation.[10] If this is the case, what is it that psychoanalysis has been claiming to do with its notion of interpretation?

Psychoanalysis has presented itself in its various forms throughout its hundred-year history as fundamentally a science or art, a practice, of interpretation. Traditional interpretive science sought the stable origin of meaning in sources exterior to the person searching: formerly, the most prevalent interpretive science, biblical hermeneutics, referenced that meaning in God's intention; the scientific discourse of modernity seeks its origin in laws ascribable to nature; astrology seeks its origin in the atomistic and perfectly determined state of the universe. Freud's revolution, which like all revolutions had its forerunners and prophets, was to seek the origin of meaning within the human, in a place—and we must use the term advisedly, for the topological dimensions can be misleading[11]—he called the unconscious. We must further specify, for if the origin of meaning were merely to be found in the human, one could claim that anatomical sciences had done a pretty good job of this already. The trick to psychoanalysis is that the origin of meaning is sought in the seeker, in the source of the question.

Dasein is that being for whom its being is a question, said Heidegger,[12] and the dimension of psychoanalysis's questioning must be located within the being-in-question that is specific to the being of Dasein. Psychoanalysts and theorists engage in interpretation and at times they suggest ways of interpreting—methods and strategies for eking out a meaning that is hidden under the surface. If we locate the dimension of psychoanalysis's quest for meaning within the being-in-question that is specific to the being of Dasein, however, then the questioning of that quest entails ultimately a dialogue—a bipolar logos, the shuttling back and forth or the borrowing and lending of the word—within Dasein itself. Indeed it would seem that Dasein, insofar as its being is in question for it, would be nothing other than the instantiation of this borrowing and lending—the instantiation of interpretation.[13]

Interpretation, then, is not the application of a technique of divination to a dormant, monologic being. Both the beings who are analyzed and those who are not analyzed are already engaged in interpretation, consciously or unconsciously.[14] If it goes on without the aid or focus of one's being conscious of it, then might this not be a way of describing the unconscious? The unconscious is the constitutive interpretation of a being whose being is a question for itself, but whose self-questioning, and hence interpretation, is a disturbance or threat to its socially established existence. Why do we add the second clause? Why is the shuttling back and forth of interpretation a disturbance or threat to socially established existence? What is, in fact, socially established existence that it should feel threatened by such a shuttling? Heidegger would call such existence inauthentic (*uneigentlich*). Freud, for his part, would likely call it neurotic, but the essence of his discovery was that most of us exist in such a way that our public selves, the selves that we display to others and that we honestly believe to be our own, are constructed as defense systems against the shuttling of interpretation. Freud called this defense system the ego, and the clinical problems psychoanalysis sought to redress he interpreted as the result of failures in the ego's attempts to cover over the shuttling of interpretation. Of course Freud did not use these exact words, and neither did Heidegger, although his terminology may have come closer. Heidegger called this shuttling *Angst*, as did Kierkegaard before him;[15] Freud thought deeply about the issue, and although the id has become one of the most overdetermined of contemporary intellectual termini, the word he chose for it in German was merely *es*, it.

The temptation of any system of thought or practice is to systematize and stabilize, and psychoanalysis is certainly no exception. Yet it can only be salutary to "return" to the texts that have founded such a system and read them, interpret them anew. Is the id really everything we have been taught to think of it as? Does interpretation really reduce everything to "daddy-mommy-me," or does it have to?[16] A hypothesis I would like to pursue in this work is that, despite their well-publicized animosity, there is nothing guaranteeing the distance between psychoanalysis and deconstruction, and much that speaks for its diminution, if not disappearance. For if the narrative I have presented so far has any validity, then the conclusion might be forecast as follows: the truth of psychoanalysis is nothing other than deconstruction, and vice versa.

Wo es war, soll ich werden—where it was must I become. Yet is this a statement of methodology, a prediction, or a neutral description of process? If it is methodological, then I, as reader, as interpreter, should follow *its* trace, wherever *it* may lead me. If *it* is interpretation, then the traces it leaves are the traces of interpretation, words that activate and react with my own as the unconscious opens briefly, only to recede again (or is the unconscious, as Lacan stipulated, the very movement of this opening and closing?). If it is a prediction, then what it tells me is that the formation of my self will always be built up over the ruins of interpretation and that this process is eternal. If it is merely description, then what is described is the urgency of the *soll*, the "ought," that lies on the border between the institution of the ego and the dissolution of interpretation, and what we could call the ethical dimension becomes inescapable for psychoanalysis. This last description, in its apparent neutrality, is the most explosive of all, for it holds the key to understanding the motive force of the ethical and the relation of desire to meaning. All three interpretations are of importance, but it is the last that will mostly guide our search.

What most concerned Kierkegaard in his elaboration of the concept of faith was that the human subject is condemned to a paradoxical relation with knowledge, or mediation. The simple form of the paradox is that the medium of knowledge is universal (i.e., transindividual), while the individual is irredeemably particular. The individual will always be required to communicate, for example, its motivations at a universal, or (what Kierkegaard calls) ethical level, and will always ultimately fail because the relation to the mediated will inevitably produce an excess of immediacy that cannot be processed by the universal. This is what he called the paradox of mediation, and he famously insisted that this paradox itself cannot be mediated.

What is of interest in the present context is that the very deconstructive insight that animates the reading of texts cannot fail to find there, in the very resistance to mediation that the paradox of mediation poses, the aporetic grounding of the distinction that the disciplines of psychoanalysis and deconstruction hold dear. To put it in simple terms, if deconstruction has emphasized the unlimited nature of mediation, its endless dissemination, and has been suspicious of psychoanalysis for the pretension with which it authorizes certain endpoints to this cascade, and if psychoanalytic thinkers have insisted on the inexorability of the signifying cut, of the real as that which always returns to the same place, all the while criticizing deconstruction for its failure to recognize the power of this desire, then Kierkegaard's refrain that the paradox of mediation cannot be mediated suggests that in their opposition each discourse contains the truth of the other. The paradox of mediation is precisely that it is limitless, pure dissemination, yet it is precisely this paradox that is the ultimate stop, the grounding cut, the abyss that cannot be mediated.

E's point

This is why we should not be surprised by the curious digressions Kierkegaard presents in the context of Johannes de Silencio's various attempts in *Fear and Trembling* to reconstruct Abraham's willingness to sacrifice Isaac in a way that could make sense or could be communicable.[17] In each case the narrator inserts a paragraph in which he compares that attempt to another strategy for weaning a child. Thus Abraham, who says to Isaac in the very act of killing him that this is his own desire and not God's, for "it is better that he believes me a monster than that he should lose faith in you," is contrasted to the mother who blackens her breast, to which the narrator adds, "How fortunate the one who did not need more terrible means to wean the child" (*FT* 11). That refrain continues, leaving no doubt but that what is at stake is nothing other than the fundamental inadequacy of each method of weaning to fully account for, justify, or communicate what for the child is an incomprehensibly terrible experience of loss. In the same way, Johannes de Silencio's several versions of Abraham can never entirely account for and hence communicate the reason for his act.

Is it not precisely here where we can point yet again to the reductive tendencies of the psychoanalytically inclined, who will always, no matter the particularities of the case at hand, locate the origin of the drive for meaning in the mother's body or in some body part, such as the original lost object, the breast? Here, however, the crucial move is in fact the opposite one: the impossibility of completely weaning the child, the persistence of a traumatic remainder to any process of separation, and so on, is not the *meaning* of Johannes de Silencio's text nor is it the answer or explanation to the impossibility of communicating Abraham's speech. The child is a victim not of "nature" but of *deconstruction*. It is not the breast or the mother's body he or she misses but rather the assurance of an ultimate explanation, the solidity of signification, and an answer that will ground his or her endless quest for self-knowledge. The traumatic kernel at the heart of our fantasy constructions, the impossible real that always returns, all of these psychoanalytic formulations that so disturb deconstructivists—these are nothing other than further failed attempts to signify the traumatic truth that is nothing other than deconstruction itself: that at the core of being is not monologic self-identity but rather the endless shifting of the bipolar logos we have been calling interpretation.

The Awakening

One of the most common sources for the current suspicion, or rather dismissal, of psychoanalysis by a majority of psychologists, researchers, and in general intellectuals is the apparent absurdity of the claim, central to Freud's methodology, that a dream represents the fulfillment of a wish.[18] What contemporary dream researchers find absurd in this claim is that it seems to identify an ultimately nonconfirmable entity, the unconscious, with its various desires at the origin and cause of a phenomenon that can be and, in the hundred years since Freud first penned the *Interpretation of Dreams*, has been demonstrated to have other confirmable causes. In more recent work the unconscious simply can be assumed to have no purpose or function, and to be "the accidental by-product" of evolutionary adaptation (Domhoff 6).[19] Why believe in a phantom unconscious when we can demonstrate that dreams have other, more tangible causes or functions or none at all? Whatever the efficient or teleological cause (function) of dreams is, however, it is ultimately irrelevant to whether or not they mean anything and to what they mean if they do.

This is not to say that the relation between dream content and potential efficient causes for dreams are not of interest. Let us look at one deceitfully simple instantiation, which Freud quotes from Jessen: "Accumulations of semen lead to lascivious dreams."[20] The science behind this assertion might be phrased somewhat as follows: males produce semen in continuation; the accumulation of semen requires occasional ejaculation; should ejaculation not occur through normal means at normal intervals, whatever these might be, a "need" develops, an internal stimulus analogous to thirst or to external stimuli such as produce an irritation of skin. The former analogue causes the subject to respond by drinking to quench the thirst, the latter to scratch in order to ease the itch. The normal response to our case example would assuredly be copulation with an available female, but given the social mores of Victorian Vienna such availability might be more or less feasible, and the stimulus, lacking other socially acceptable forms of response, might be left to accumulate to the point where it interferes with the subject's sleep.

In our two analogous cases, the thirsty sleeper might respond to his or her thirst by dreaming of a cold glass of water, in which case the "meaning" of the dream can be chalked up to thirst. Similarly, the itchy sleeper might respond by dreaming of a cool chamomile bath or of some other form of epidermal soothing, and the meaning of the dream would be the itch. In the case of our semen-accumulating subject, the dream might be an erotic one resulting in what are known as nocturnal emissions and the meaning of the dream may be classified as a carnal urge. The meaning, of course, remains the same whatever the manifestation of, organization of, or ultimately content of the dream is, as long as the dream is one of drinking, soothing, or being erotic, and we are assured of this because we know that the subject in question suffers from the observed stimuli. We know, in other words, what we are looking for before we have begun.

What I am suggesting with this *reductio* of causal explanations is that the goal of the quest into the meaning of a dream remains unfulfilled by reference to a stimulus cause, for the stimulus cause is itself ultimately meaningless because it is apparently free to cause or not to cause a dream of a given kind and has absolutely nothing to say about the specific dream that results, should it indeed succeed in causing one to occur. "Scientific inquiry," Freud says, "however, cannot stop there [at the objective sensory stimulus]. It finds an occasion for further questions in the observed fact that the stimulus that impinges on the senses during sleep does not appear in its real shape but is replaced by another image in some way related to it" (*ID* 61). Not only could seminal retention *not* have resulted in a dream accompanying nocturnal emissions, but if such a dream did occur, the seminal retention, had it indeed taken place, tells us nothing about the dream or why it was erotic to that particular person. All of this ignores the most obvious disproof of the causal thesis: the example of seminal retention would seem to require that women never have erotic dreams.

The refutation of such drivel is hardly of intellectual interest. Nevertheless, Freud's argument opens a fascinating path of inquiry, namely, what is the nature of the relation between stimulus causes and the images that replace them in the dream? Freud's evocation of Schopenhauer is instructive: according to the philosopher, all knowledge is in a relation to sensory input such that the impressions received from the senses are molded into the "forms of space, time, and causality," a notion Schopenhauer has from Kant, for whom space and time are the necessary forms of all intuition and causality is applicable exclusively to the phenomenal realm.[21] Sensory impulses, in other words, come from outside but are only knowable in their phenomenal form as occurring within space and time and having been synthesized according to laws of causality. The difference between diurnal cognition and nocturnal cognition is reduced to information volume: internal stimuli normally drowned out by the diurnal cacophony are themselves subjected to the ordering of space, time, and causality and present themselves as dreams. What is of interest in this description, and what clearly attracted Freud, is the idea that the meaning of the dream need not be located in the specific causal stimuli but rather in the processes by which these stimuli are transformed into recognizable images for us—how, for example, the stimulus of thirst is transformed into a particular series of images is of central importance. "The sensation that has been aroused evokes a cognate image, in accordance with some law of association" (*ID* 71). This law, then, must be the subject of any attempt at developing an interpretive method.

Freud turns to a notion taken from the hermeneuticist Friedrich Schleiermacher for help in resolving this question of the law. For Schleiermacher, "what characterizes the waking state is that thought-activity takes place in concepts and not in images" (*ID* 82). Images, however, in Freud's interpretation need not be limited to visual images although they are predominantly visual. What is characteristic of dreams is that they are experienced as though lived, as though perceived via the senses, and hence are what we might call imaginary in that their language is one of images and not concepts. Of course concepts have their place in dreams as well, as when one dreams of a conversation—in which imaginary words convey concepts—or dreams that one reads a text. The problem with this formulation is that it ceases to be distinguished from lived experience per se, in which we can also say that imaginary words convey concepts. This is why Freud can say, "in agreement with every authority on the subject, that dreams hallucinate—that they replace thoughts by hallucinations" (*ID* 82). Hallucination is invoked precisely because its primary characteristic is that it can be indistinguishable from reality, for, as Freud says at another point, the only moment at which the dreamer is positively aware that the experience is dreamed and not really experienced is the moment of passage to the new reality—that is, the awakening (*ID* 84).

Most would tend to disagree with this assertion, citing the many times they, and presumably all of us, are aware of dreaming and aware of being aware that the dream is a dream. Nevertheless, the philosophical point is recognizable to us as one of the key ingredients in the conundrums typical of modern, that is, Cartesian, epistemology. How can I know that what my senses present to me is real? I cannot know it with certainty because perhaps I am dreaming.[22] This dream metaphor as skeptical foundation has been central to not a few great works of literature. Perhaps the most influential of these works is Calderon de la Barca's *Life Is a Dream*, in which the protagonist never actually dreams but is merely convinced that at one waking moment he is in fact dreaming.[23] On the basis of this experience, he learns to govern his own behavior via the fear that at any moment he could awake from what is in truth nothing but a dream.

The evidence for our faith in the realistic nature of dreams, then, has nothing to do with their realism or believability. This faith ultimately rests not on the content (in fact the content of the experience is what tells us constantly that there is no way this is real) but on the position of the subject experiencing. What pertains to the level of representation is experienced at the level of presentations. To put it another way, "we appear not to think but to experience" (*ID* 83), but what we are experiencing is thought.

The transformations between stimulus and image would thus seem to correspond to another mode of transformation, that between image and idea or between experience and thought. To review: a given physical or organic stimulus may be responsible for provoking a dream scenario in the form of a series of images. The images are in turn experienced at the level of lived or sensory reality—but presumably unlike lived experience, this reality can be unmasked at any time by the awakening, a revelation that the sensory experience was not lived but was something else, something in relation to a lived reality—something like stimuli, which, however, can themselves not be experienced in any form outside of the sensory or the "forms of space, time, and causality." The dream images are thus marked by a certain liminality: they are sensory experience that has been refuted, displaced in light of something real that lies beyond.

What pertains to the level of representation is experienced at the level of presentation, a phrasing that also indicates a shift only made possible or realized by the awakening, the coming out of the dream or the liminality that marks the dream image. To push this thought another step further would take us to the apparently paradoxical notion that the awakening, or the coming out of the dream, is not an exit that leaves behind the world of images while revealing them to have been representations but is rather constitutive of their essence as dream images. The dream only becomes the dream at the moment of the awakening, at the moment when it enters into a relation with thought or concepts. The order of analysis, the temporality of analysis, then, is inverted. It is not that physical/organic stimuli produce dream images that are recognized as such in the awakening; rather, the awakening emerges and distinguishes itself as thought against the fading of dream images, which it interprets as the impingements of a reality from which it thought it had taken flight. Yet the impingement is itself an *interpretation*, carried out by the dreamer without his or her knowledge, or an interpretation fundamental to having knowledge of a self or even to having a self of whom to have knowledge. This interpretation, necessarily lost or written over in the annals of the awakening, is exactly of the same order as the interpretation of the awakening; it is of the order of that thought that bears witness to an imaginary world or a world of images, only deciding in the moment of its foundation which of those it is. It is therefore of the order of putting-into-words, of naming and narrating that which of itself is unnamed and unnarrated—namely, bare stimuli. The imaginary is born of the naming of the world, but it is a second birth, the awakening, that releases the imaginary into the world.

In dreaming, or in awakening to the memory of dreams, we are witnessing bare naming, or language stripped of the coherence of its usage in socially constrained, pragmatic ways. Furthermore, our witnessing, from the perspective of the thoughts of the awakening, takes the form of "having experienced," and there is much evidence that suggests that the pastness of this experience should provoke suspicion, as when the dreamer relates an entire adventure that seems to lead up to the pealing of bells that "turn out to be" his or her dream's interpretation of an alarm clock. What can we make of such remarkable compression? Perhaps that the very pastness of the experience is part of the creative act of the awakening, because if dream images are to be experienced instead of thought, they can only ever be thought of as already experienced; for thought, experience is always in the past. The experience that was the dream, then, is conjured in its pastness in the present of the awakening. The awakening, in turn, is the coming into coherence of thoughts, the aligning of them with a sense of self that is centered in an already fading moment of time. The coming into coherence leaves in its wake an incoherence of thoughts, which the awakening recalls as having been its stimuli, its imaginary. The dream images, then, are in truth also thoughts: there arise "in the mind in the first place a number of ideas, which are represented in the form of hallucinations or more properly . . . of illusions, in view of their derivation from external and internal stimuli" (*ID* 91). The images are illusions insofar as they are not identical to the stimuli from which they derive but also because they are not identical to the ideas that they in fact are, for it is also clear that an idea and an image cannot be identical. The ideas "become linked according to the familiar laws of association and, according to these same laws, call up a further series of ideas (or images)" (*ID* 91). Here we see the first great and lasting insight of the *Interpretation*: the dream content is composed of networks of ideas, concepts, in short, words, relating to one another via laws of association (which we will now recognize as the movements along the syntagmatic and paradigmatic axes classified for the purposes of literary and linguistic analysis by structuralism), which are (will have been) perceived or remembered to have been perceived by the subject at the moment of the awakening. On one level they are representations perceived as presentations, but on another level they are productions (*ID* 116) that are interpreted as reproductions. What this discovery now points to or the question it now raises is that of motivation: what drives the dreamer to produce just this set of images in his or her interpretation?

Templates of Freud's method had been in circulation since antiquity. Dream books from various cultures presented the interpreter with code keys that indicated translations for given recurrent images in dreams, the same sort of relief from obscurity promised on the press copy of the Avon paperback edition of the *Interpretation of Dreams*. The codebooks make it clear that the key to the hidden coherence of dream images is the fact that the image is an imagistic rendering of a concept, which when revealed as that concept is allowed to enter into relations with other concepts heretofore unseen, according to the logic of a rebus. "The fact that these connections inevitably disappear in translation accounts for the unintelligibility of the renderings in our own popular dream books" (*ID* 131), which, motivated by an exoticizing orientalism, have slavishly transcribed the codes of other cultures and languages without disclosing that the justification for the application of these codes could exist only within the context of the original language. Freud's leap from these extant modes of dream interpretation was to locate the origin of the code not in a language or culture but in an individual, hence at the same time annulling its value as a stable and translatable code and replacing it with a process so unstable, so fungible as to lose all possibility of independent verification outside of the individual himself. If psychoanalysis solves the riddle of human dreaming, it can only do so at the cost of its own pretensions to scientificity. Rather than merely relegating the practice to the obscurity of art or religion, however, we see in this sacrifice of independent verification a truth concerning the work of interpretation as it occurs in all knowledge-creative processes. At the most fundamental level interpretation concerns the encounter between the particular and the universal, or the universalization of particular experience, and as such unavoidably invokes a kernel of faith, a bedrock of absolute decisiveness on the border of the undecidable. It is a point of absolute obscurity from the perspective of systematic knowledge, which Freud alludes to at various points, such as when he refers to the "obscurity in which the center of our being . . . is veiled from our knowledge," which tallies with "the obscurity surrounding the origin of dreams" too well not to be brought into relation with each other (*ID* 69). As he says at another point, "There is at least one spot in every dream at which it is unplumbable—a navel, as it were, that is its point of contact with the unknown" (*ID* 143). Interpretation is fundamentally creative insofar as at the core of its movements, its associations, operates a trope as metaphysical as it is poetic (indeed, the metaphysical is nothing other than this trope): namely, metaphor, or the point at which thought emerges from the abyss.[24]

How then does the method function? What occurs when we treat "the dream itself as a symptom" and insert it "into the psychical chain that has to be traced backwards in the memory from a pathological idea" (*ID* 133)? By inserting the dream image into a network of ideas culled from the patient's own narratives, the analyst attempts to tally the dream, or bring it into relation with a world of "time, space, and causality," thereby establishing a relation with something outside that relation, something refusing to fit. The origin in the present of the chain is a "pathological idea," and if we take this at its word as a Kantian notion we find that this present, idea, or thought is pathological not only insofar as it participates in a symptomatic suffering or pathos but also insofar as it is pathetic, or passive in its relation to other phenomena, and hence in Kantian terms heteronomous as opposed to autonomous. The idea with which we start, in other words, is trapped in a causal relation to the world. By bringing it into relation with the dream images—born of the awakening into precisely that causal, coherent world—we initiate a chain of associations that leads us to a point of insertion into phenomenality, into pathology, the point of naming, of autonomy, of freedom. Our pathology is our refusal of freedom, which is the same as our refusal to interpret interpretation, which is the same as our refusal to recognize interpretation for what it is. In Freud's words: "In the state used for the analysis of dreams and pathological ideas, the patient purposely and deliberately abandons this activity [one 'which we allow to influence the course of our ideas while we are awake'] and employs the psychical energy thus saved (or a portion of it) in attentively following the involuntary thoughts which now emerge, and which—and here the situation differs from that of falling asleep—retain the character of ideas. *In this way the 'involuntary' ideas are transformed into 'voluntary' ones*" (*ID* 134–35). Falling asleep, in other words, also involves a relaxation of the deliberate activity of influencing the course of our ideas such that we might claim that the course of our ideas is *liberated* from the authority of our *deliberation*, but in sleep this process transforms those ideas into images. This brings us to posit that it is the heteronomous influence of our deliberation that prevents ideas not only from coursing freely but also from presenting themselves, that is, from being experienced as real. The relaxation of this de-liberation allows them free flow but also allows them to resolve into images, which according to the above logic are not really free because what one experiences is necessarily experienced as involuntary (e.g., if I fall into a pool it is not a matter of choice whether I experience the water as wet). By allowing the free flow of the ideas while forcing them to retain their character as ideas and not allowing them to resolve into dream images, the analysis permits them a liberty to flow free from deliberation without simultaneously enabling the constraints on their freedom characteristic of the involuntary image. An idea must be produced, must be created, and its creation is its freedom.

This leads us at last to the most provocative, infamous, and controversial aspect of Freud's theory of dreams: his contention that "When the work of interpretation has been completed, we perceive that a dream is the fulfillment of a wish" (*ID* 154). The obvious reason that this formulation has sparked such controversy is well documented in Freud's own text: how can such an assertion stand against the universal experience of unpleasant dreams when the apparent definition of a wish is that it be for something pleasant, as in provoking feelings of pleasure and not pain? This well-known aspect of Freud's theory ultimately resulted in his criticizing and eventually debunking that very notion of a wish. Indeed, the primary and secondary processes he outlines in the *Interpretation of Dreams*, as in the *Project for a Scientific Psychology* before it, are already the cornerstones of a theoretical edifice denying the identity of the pleasurable and the desirable. What we must retain for the current discussion, however, is merely that in identifying the fulfillment of a wish as the centerpiece of a dream interpretation, he is revising not only our received notions of the meaning and interpretation of dreams but also and more fundamentally the meaning of our very notion of desire. If, in other words, our dreams when interpreted reveal the fulfillment of a wish, it is also the case that *wish* can be defined as that the fulfillment of which is revealed by the *interpretation* of a dream.

To grasp this point we need first to turn to Freud's explanations and strategies for presenting even the most unpleasant dreams, nightmares, "distressing dreams and anxiety-dreams" (*ID* 168), as somehow fulfilling wishes. The trope lies in his distinction between a dream's manifest and latent content. The principal criticism of this distinction should not be too easily dismissed: once we have identified two contents, one of which by definition is not readily apparent, then we have constructed a largely self-confirming theory, once again incapable of independent confirmation because the latent content can only ever be revealed by an interpretation, probably our own. When we add the notion of "resistance" to this distinction, we have achieved the armature of infallibility usually limited to religious apparatuses, as even the patient's misgivings as to an interpreted latent content may be dismissed as being motivated by the same socially conditioned forces that relegated the content to its latent position in the first place. Once again, psychoanalysis has proven itself incompatible with the standards of proof necessary for modern science.

The greater danger deriving from the manifest-latent distinction, however, is that it will be interpreted, as it largely has been, as positing the existence of a layer or locality of wishes unpalatable to the public self, whose ultimate revelation through psychoanalysis releases the subject from the symptomatic pressure produced by the latent wish in its urge to find expression. I venture that this description would be welcomed by many practicing psychoanalysts, who would find my objection to it odd. On the contrary, my resistance to this notion grows from the conviction that Freud's formulation of the nature of dreams was equally a formulation of the nature of desire.

First, the idea of two contents, one veiling the other, is immediately disavowed via the notion of distortion, for the manifest content of a dream is not another competing content but rather the distortion of the latent content via the dream work. In the case of Freud's dream of his friend R. in which R. appears as Freud's uncle, we are presented with no fewer than four levels of interpretation. First, there was presumably a dream that was experienced as presented, not represented. Second, there is a first representation of that dream in a written form (and here we skip a step which might be called the immediate recollection of the dream upon awakening). Third, there is the interpretation of the written dream. Finally, in this case, there is a footnote commenting on and interpreting the interpretation of the dream. Far from suggesting that the dream itself (and much less its manifest content) has a self-sufficient status as the fulfillment of a wish, Freud's methodology reveals again and again what his definition states in so many words: "When the work of interpretation has been completed, we perceive that a dream is the fulfillment of a wish"; in other words, this perception comes about only through the process of interpretation. In the case of Freud's friend R., the four levels of interpretation reveal themselves to be nothing other than the story of the distortion, or interpretation, of a wish. The wish that Freud's case for promotion be seen independently of the denominational reasons—their Judaism—that ultimately explained the failure of both R. and Uncle Joseph to win promotions does not exist independently of the very series of associations that lead him to it but is rather an ideational translation, interpretation, or distortion of dream images that are retroactively born of that very process of awakening that leads to the recollection of the dream as having been experienced. At every step of the way, microtransformations occur along the liminal border between images and ideas, and at each of these points desire is evinced, desire that can equally and at the same time produce images of beauty and repulsion, of goodness and evil, of nobility and baseness. What this desire-lineage reveals is precisely the self's ethical boundary. The borderline defining the acceptable and unacceptable for the symbolic constellation of a given personality is played out repeatedly, in myriad forms and formulations, in the transformation between ideas and dream images and back again.

As Freud's comments regarding children and their dreams suggest, the distinction between the manifest and the latent has yet to be established in full, given that the censoring functions that help construct the border distinguishing the two, or the event line of transformation, to be more accurate, are not yet fully instituted. Yet what we observe in children is not so much the unbridled or bare form of what will later become latent contents as the unproblematic co-existence of what would appear to be mutually conflicting desires, and which would for that reason seem to require the manifest-latent distinction. For example, already at two-and-a-half my son loved to watch *The Lion King*, and his favorite character was the villain Scar although he was terrified of Scar to the point of leaving the room whenever Scar entered the scene. Nevertheless, when the television was off, his request took the form of a plaintive "Scar?" When asked if Scar is good or bad, he replied without hesitation, "bad"; but when asked if he likes Scar, he also replied without hesitation that he did.

Given this interpretation, Freud's elucidation of the relation between the primary and secondary systems, between the pleasure principle and the reality principle, between the unconscious and consciousness, can be understood as aligning along the same axis. The primary and secondary systems cannot be conceived of as independent agencies but are rather each the necessary counterpart of the other, and thoughts and desires are not confined to one or the other agency but occur or are produced via the transformations between them. If Freud insists that "Nothing, it would seem, can reach consciousness from the first system without passing the second" (*ID* 177), this is true because the two systems are not separate systems but different sides of the same process or passing. If we say "that distressing dreams do in fact contain something which is distressing to the *second* agency, but something which at the same time fulfills a wish on the part of the *first* agency" (*ID* 179), it is neither a correction nor a contradiction but rather an interpretation, in the true sense of the word, to insist that the something, being inseparable from its manifestation in either agency, is nothing other than the transformation between agencies itself. It is a transformation that is simultaneously distressing and wish-fulfilling without entering into contradiction; moreover, it can be concluded from this that the agencies themselves are brought into existence only by the very distinction that grants them their identity, a distinction that itself derives from nothing other than the transformation in question. This transformation we have been calling interpretation, and if psychoanalysis proposes a method, also called interpretation, the purpose of that method can only be described as a vigilance over and a tracing of the movements and transformation of desire.

The Fault-Line

When one speaks of the major critiques of psychoanalysis and psychoanalytic thinking (that is, those critiques that it behooves psychoanalysis to take seriously), deconstruction, Deleuzian philosophy, and Foucault's discourse analysis must take first rank. Foucault's critique is of a historico-political nature, arguing that psychoanalytic practice takes part in and in fact enables the production of the very symptoms it purports to be curing, discursively producing sexuality, its repression, and its resultant symptoms as objects of analysis, because it partakes in and is in some way exemplary of a culture in which sexuality as the object of intimate confession is consistently positioned as the ultimate bearer of a subject's interior truth. To take an appropriate historical example, by agreeing to take as an object of study the so-called perversions, psychoanalysis joins the other sexological practices of the time in creating an essential distinction between normal and abnormal sexuality.[25] Foucauldian analysis aims at revealing the constructed nature of such distinctions in the hopes that such a revelation will dissipate the categories and hence perhaps some of the social harms they have produced.

The Foucauldian analysis, then, takes the form of declaring historically contingent certain categories that psychoanalysis, so it claims, has helped create. In this sense, the critical practice may be called epistemological because it has to do with categories of knowledge, although it clearly emphasizes that a certain lived reality is produced by these categories of knowledge.[26] Nevertheless, what this epistemological criticism fails to take into account is the reflective nature of the categories of knowledge themselves. The category of perversions, for example, is dismissed as establishing an arbitrary distinction between one group of disparate sexual practices deemed normal and another deemed abnormal or perverse. While there is nothing inherent to the group of excluded practices that justifies their exclusion, however, there is one thing they all have in common: they are and have been recognized as perversions, even by the people practicing them, and this commonality could well be one important factor in their appeal.

Deconstruction and the thought of Deleuze and Guattari share with Foucault the concern that there is something limiting or constraining about psychoanalytic practice, but the domain of their interrogation lies largely in the assumptions underlying psychoanalysis as an interpretive practice. In the former case, deconstruction takes psychoanalysis to task on the issue of interpretive authority, noting that psychoanalysis tends to found its interpretive reductions on some ultimately unquestionable authority, whether it is the authority of psychoanalytic masters or, in the work of the master himself, on the authority of clinical experience.[27] In the latter case, Deleuze and Guattari accuse psychoanalysis as being a tool for the normalization of subjects in that its interpretive methodology consists of replacing multiple forms of enjoyment (that is, of desire) with one foundational model of desire exemplified in the myth of Oedipus (*AO* 53). What is common to both critiques is that the interpretive practice of psychoanalysis is seen as reductive and normalizing and hence inimical to expressions of both social and textual freedom.

It is my sense that, although the grounds for such complaints are everywhere evident, psychoanalytic texts need not be read in such a fashion. Indeed, as Barbara Johnson argued in her contribution to the "Purloined Letter" debate, to read these texts in this way closes them off in a precisely analogous way to how the deconstructive and Deleuzian critics claim psychoanalysis closes off its alternative readings.[28] Freud's own texts contain the seeds of an entirely different notion of interpretation than his critics have claimed, and if we are truly interested in promoting such dynamic, creative, and productive modes of reading, then it makes sense to read deliberately for them rather than merely seek repressive enemies to provide backdrops for our own liberating readings.

If what we are seeking is an entirely different notion of interpretation than what tends to be passed down through either critical readings or a diffuse popular Freudianism, this notion will necessarily take the shape of something other than Freudianism in its mythical form. The mythical form is transmitted through pithy sayings and facile formulations, many of which can certainly be traced to Freud: the boy's desire is to marry his mother and murder his father, biology is destiny, and a variety of other quotables that allow Freud to be tossed away as easily as they are tossed off. Yet if the "something other" to which I would like to pay heed is there, then it must inhere in Freud's words even in the way the dream thoughts inhere in the dream content—inhere, that is, as an exigency of reading that repeats itself and expands through and against every attempt to put it to rest with a final word.

Read in this light, the *Interpretation of Dreams* is not about how to interpret in the sense of replacing the rich text of a dream with another, reduced and normalized version; rather, it is about another Freudian notion, still rich despite interminable attempts to give it a determinate, settled, and ultimately terminal meaning: the unconscious. As Deleuze and Guattari themselves say, the unconscious remains Freud's greatest invention, and one they wish to rescue from Oedipus (*AO* 24). To put the discussion around the unconscious into another framework—one alien to the popular and reductive reception of it as a place beyond the reach of the light of consciousness—let us consider that what Freud identifies as the unconscious at work in the latent content of dreams is nothing other than the possibility that a dream (or text) has of meaning something other than what it says, a literary trope identified with the device of irony and a quality Lacan claimed for the signifier itself (*E* 155). Furthermore, because the ego's proper role is that of, along with the belated super-ego, carrying on the censorship of that material emerging from the dream thought and thereby effecting distortions that lead to its manifest form, the practice of reading for latent content could certainly not be classified along with intentionalist readings of literary texts, for here what is "meant" is clearly not what the author as ego meant, but the author as something else, as "it," insofar as our reading is that rubbing of the vase that releases the genie inside.

The dreamer is still implicated in the meaning of the dream, of course, but no longer as far as his or her intention is concerned but rather as far as his or her desire is concerned, which is of an entirely different stripe, for desire has now also suffered a violent redefinition and no longer coincides with what the ego thinks it wants but is rather always something else, something other. Desire is that which finds itself fulfilled in dream, which is precisely one of those statements that provoked Deleuze and Guattari's ire because it appeared to separate desire from reality—although of course Lacan has always insisted on the real, if not the *reality*, of desire. Realities can indeed be lacking in reality insofar as they avoid desire or try to sate it with something permanent; for desire is only insatiable insofar as to sate implies to bring to a stop whereas desire is always in motion. Desire is that which finds itself fulfilled isn a dream, as interpreted, because the interpretation reveals the dream to be the minimum movement between at least two ideas trapped, as it were, in the memory of an image.

Perhaps this is why Freud constantly refers to the quality dreams have of combining stimuli or ideas: "Many experiences such as this lead me to assert that the dream-work is under some kind of necessity of combining all the sources which have acted as stimuli for the dream in the dream itself"; or, "If in the course of a single day we have two or more experiences suitable for provoking a dream, the dream will make a combined reference to them as a single whole; *it is under a necessity to combine them into a unity*" (*ID* 211–12). The ability to combine into a unity, to make one of two, would seem to be eminently a property of the signifier. To put it in the terms of classical semiotics, "a sign is that which refers itself to something else," that which resonates with the literary idiom of Borges, who never ceased to be astonished that the verb "to cleave" in English could mean at the same time to rend and to adhere.[29] To insist in the disputed language of Hegelian dialectics that the signifier, like language, "has the divine nature of directly reversing the meaning of what is said, of making it into something else, and thus not letting what is meant get into words at all" (Hegel 66) certainly runs the risk of raising Deleuzian hackles and having the speaker classified among the priests of lack.[30] Yet the very opacity that infests signification provides the motor of communicative practice, and the specter of lack must be qualified with the knowledge that *not* being something invariably leads to *being* something else.

My suspicion is that Freud's discovery leads us to the following conclusion: lived experience provokes a steady stream of interpretation into thought, which invariably presents conscious experience—which must deal with the conditions of universality brought about by rational communication, decision making, corroboration of experience, and so on—with an endless series of choices. Images/experiences branch off into a variety of thought-virtualities, and thought units branch into further thought sequences. When Freud insists that something from a given day's experiences lends itself to instigating a dream, that "the freshness of an impression gives it some kind of psychical value for purposes of dream construction" (*ID* 214), the interpretation that suggests itself is that the dream in fact begins to unravel a string knitted during that day's exercise of rational thought. The composition of that string depended upon the continuous rejection of thought-virtualities in accordance with a self-image whose implicit daily activity involves the careful maintenance of a somewhat consistent and recognizable ethical boundary. If we recall that de-liberation, or reflective judgment, may be considered as the faculty responsible for preventing the "free flow" of ideas (namely, that flow or unknitting that would result once the strictures of reason allowed thought to flow into its constitutive tributaries), then we will also not fail to notice that it is precisely this reflective distance that permits thoughts to remain thoughts, that is, to be experienced as representative reflection and not lived presentations. Hence, when this de-liberative distance is relaxed, we tend to fall into a servitude of another kind, for the flow of thoughts resolves into images that we experience as sensory or memory presentations. As should be clear by now, these presentations are signifiers and retain that quality of signifiers to mean something other than what they say, and therefore the cascade that this relaxation of de-liberation instigates is a kind of decompression or de-composition whose traces are to be followed in the interpretation. The unconscious is not, then, what is discovered *by* this process; rather, it is that which is discovered *in and through* this process; it is the *spacing* between liberation and the de-liberation that tries to follow its traces. Why this is of importance is that the path it traces concerns us at the most fundamental level of our desire.

Freud's readings of his own dreams and those of his patients in the *Interpretation of Dreams* tend to place a certain emphasis on latent contents of a sexual nature and on lost memories from childhood, two aspects that will now require our attention. Nevertheless, a further commonality binds his account of how dreams knit together these memories and respond to hidden urges: Freud's readings invariably turn upon oppositions revealed at the heart of apparent thematic unities. For instance, toward the end of his account of his own dream about the three women in the kitchen, Freud states:

> Because this lesson of "*carpe diem*" had among other meanings a sexual one, and because the desire it expressed did not stop short of doing wrong, it had reason to dread the censorship and was obliged to conceal itself behind a dream. All kinds of thoughts having a *contrary* sense then found voice: memories of a time when the dreamer was content with spiritual food, restraining thoughts of every kind and even threats of the most revolting sexual punishments. (*ID* 241)

This sentence deserves some sustained attention. To begin with, let us release some of the rationalizing constraint of the explanatory clause. Now we are left with the claim that there was, among others, a sexual meaning to this dream and that the desire expressed does not stop short of doing wrong. If our previous line of thought has validity to it, it is not so much that these are reasons for the thoughts hiding themselves in dreams as that the very nature of the dream is to be the product of what Deleuze and Guattari would call the rhizomatic division and multiplication of thoughts and the subsequent production of rational thought through the constant dismissal or hiding of entire chains of ideas. Desire does not stop short of doing wrong precisely because and insofar as thought determines, in conjunction with a social field of expectations, the point at which wrong ends and right begins. Moreover, the apparently obsessive return of sexual themes in Freud's readings, if not the obsession with sex at the heart of dreams per se (and here differences can and must clearly be grasped in terms of changing cultural and historical norms), is because for psychoanalysis sex has definitely ceased to signify the apparatus and milieu of biological reproduction.[31] What sex has to do with is precisely desire that does not stop at doing wrong; with the shifting or translation between spiritual and profane contentments; with the line demarcating liberty from the de-liberations that constrain it and define it; and with the threats of punishment that haunt that line, ultimately only as revolting as they are enticing and hence sexual. The sexual, after psychoanalysis, is synonymous with that enjoyment that is beyond the pleasure principle, where the pleasure principle is nothing but the myth of a drivenness or being-in-the-world prior to and independent of its opposing principle, the reality principle. At the core of our identity is a fissure, a border, a unifying trait, constantly in motion, *extimate*[32] insofar as it defines our relation to otherness and the outside all the while remaining utterly intimate. This trait is at the same time an ethical fault-line because it determines those points at which we constantly draw and redraw our sense of right and because it lies at the basis of our feelings of fault, of who or what is at fault for the situation in which we find ourselves. Simultaneously, as indicated so powerfully in the French word *faute,* it marks the point of origin of an urge to transgress that underlies desire as such. Psychoanalysis, in Lacan's words from 1959, is concerned above all with *l'univers de la faute*.[33]

That the almost overwhelming presence of the sexual in psychoanalytic interpretation is explainable in terms of a different understanding of the sexual itself points us to a similar reworking of childhood memories in their connection with the practice of dream interpretation. If dreams have an immediate source in the previous day's events, they seem invariably in Freud's readings to turn on memories that are only conjured retroactively, during the succeeding analytic sessions, from the patients' distant past. In his own words, a dream is "linked in its manifest content with recent experiences and in its latent content with the most ancient experiences" (*ID* 252); or again, in dreams "a succession of meanings or wish-fulfillments may be superimposed on one another, the bottom one being the fulfillment of a wish dating from earliest childhood" (*ID* 253). Indeed, this reliance on recovered memories has provoked considerable ridicule from the critics of psychoanalysis, who maintain that it engages in the unsavory practice of producing ostensible memories of the past along with traumatic and normally sexual events, portraying them as the recovered memories of real sexual traumas. As Laplanche and Pontalis have argued,[34] however, the question of whether the seduction ever actually took place is of less concern for psychoanalysis—hence the questionable place of psychoanalysis in the courtroom—because what is at stake is a primal fantasy and its subsequent repression. The nature of these primal scenes and their value for psychoanalytic practice remain to be discussed in our context; what is important here is the status of the infantile memory: why does Freud constantly return to the distant past in his quest for meaning?

As indicated previously, the striking commonality among Freud's obsessively evoked dream etiologies is the unification of opposites, which is also in force in his deployment of child memories. In the context of his analysis of his own dream that ends with the micturition of an old man in a bottle, Freud not only invokes "the significant part played in dreams by children's difficulties in connection with micturition" but also makes the further connection to his own memory of having "disregarded the rules which modesty lays down and obeyed the calls of nature in my parents' bedroom while they were present." He recalls his father's response as having been "The boy will come to nothing," a judgment he registers as having been surely a "frightful blow to my ambition" (*ID* 250). The example is insightful because of how it stages the childhood memory as a cross-road for competing impulses or, as the language of the text has it, laws. Modesty lays down certain laws, and in doing so modesty plays the part of the one who was most likely the lawgiver in Freud's household, the very man who then issues a judgment concerning the limited nature of Freud's prospects. Facing him in his guise of modesty is another lawgiver, this time nature, personifying the urge to micturate—not elsewhere, not later, but here and now. The father and nature face off across a line in the dirt whose competing sides have been otherwise named as the reality and pleasure principles, or the primary and secondary processes; and in accordance with our reading practice we cannot fail to notice that they are of course one and the same, that there would be no father/law of modesty without its counterpart, and that nature would have no impulse to call had not modesty established itself as an obstacle. In an exactly analogous way, the father's judgment on Freud's prospects establishes a border separating success from its lack, in that very establishment defining Freud's ambition, orienting his desire in relation to it, and relegating the childhood memory of this constitutive disappointment to the ethical borderlands that feed our dreams.

The repercussions of this insight are also of interest for other aspects of Freud's theory, pointedly, for instance, for the thesis that "dreams are the *guardians* of sleep and not its disturbers" (*ID* 267), a contention that certainly may be corroborated in a somatic sense by the notion of a body's physical need for sleep but whose psychoanalytic impact would have to be sought elsewhere—for instance, in the functional service sleep provides as a vehicle for dreams. If this reversal is permissible, then dreams have an interest in guarding sleep insofar as sleep provides a vehicle for dreams— a vehicle, in other words, for the unconscious re-visitation of the ethical fault-line, of the myriad divisions and re-combinations constitutive of selfhood. In this case, the dream does not merely seek to prolong the sleep craved by the soma; rather, it is further driven in a pursuit that is desire itself. Because the path of this pursuit is by definition a kind of courting of disaster, a tightrope act between the revolting and the enticing that finds enticement only at the limits of the bearable, however, there is an immediate risk that the dream goes too far and the dreamer's sleep is disrupted, as in the case of our nightmares or anxiety dreams.

This framework can help us better understand Lacan's revision of the famous dream of the man holding vigil over his dead son's coffin. Freud understood the dream—in which the son appears before the man, asking him in reproachful terms if he cannot see that the son is burning— as the father's attempt to continue sleeping despite the evidence coming to his senses that a fire was indeed in progress and in danger of burning his son's body. Lacan's reading, in contrast, inverts the relation between sleep and desire by claiming that the father awakens in order to escape the horror of the real of his desire, namely, that he might indeed desire the burning of his son.[35] It is crucial to remember that such an absurd-sounding desire cannot be grasped outside the context of its revelation in this particular dream. The instigator of the dream is certainly the sensory evidence of the fire; the man's desire—according to Lacan and to our extrapolation of Freud's argument—is to continue dreaming so as to continue to follow the path of his desire, a path that treads the razor-sharp line dividing his son's life from his death, a father's love from its opposite, his hatred and murderous wishes. It follows, then, that the dream's exploration of this issue, no doubt also driven by the continued stimuli of flames and smoke, eventually crosses that line and gives voice to what for the father's ego is an unbearable thought, yet one just as much his own as the most tender thoughts of love. As he awakes, his fragile ego awakes, in terror at the revelation of his own desire.

In his immensely popular presentation of his theory in the *Vorlesungen* or lectures of 1915 to 1917, Freud gives several other examples explaining the phenomenon of the unpleasant or fear-provoking dream. At one point he directs the audience's attention to a well-known fairy tale in which a poor man and his wife are granted three wishes by a fairy. When the wife accidentally wishes for some bratwurst and hence wastes the first wish, her husband responds by wishing the bratwurst to hang from his wife's nose, which they promptly do. As the man and his wife represent together the figure of the wisher, the third wish can only be that the bratwurst disappear from the wife's nose, thus finishing off the three wishes and returning the couple to their original state.[36] To begin with, Freud uses the fairy tale to illustrate how a wisher can be understood to be composed of more than one agency and hence be in contradiction with himself or herself. A bit later, however, Freud pushes the point even further, arguing that in dreams the fulfillment of wishes, of fears, and of punishments can often be unified. From this we can see, he says, "that opposites [like a wish and a fear] stand especially close together in the process of association and, in the unconscious, as we have heard, they come together" (209, my translation). If we understand, as we should, a wish to be the correlate of the primary process and fear to be the correlate of the secondary process—the social opprobrium a wish can inspire—then what this example demonstrates is the fungibility of the two positions. Primary and secondary become relative values determined by their respective positions rather than given psychological phenomena.

This claim is strengthened by a reading Freud performs, in the same lecture, of a dream in which a woman describes going to the theater with her husband. Freud's interpretation of the dream turns on an association between the couple's arriving at the theater too early and the woman's having married too early: "In the present anger over her early marriage she reaches back to that time when marrying early was in fact the fulfillment of her wish, as it satisfied her voyeurism [*Schaulust*—in reference to the desire to know something of married life], and replaces, guided by the excitement of this old wish, getting married with going to the theater" (210, my translation). The crucial move here is to see how, in Freud's reading, two opposing wishes—to marry early and not to have married early—can turn out to be the expression of temporal displacement in one subject's desire. The dream, itself expressing the temporal compression typical of the unconscious, associates the two wishes and reveals them in their antagonism to be nothing other than the temporal extension of one wish: the wish to cross a line, see the other side, once acted upon is immediately haunted by the shadow wish it extrudes in the moment of its enactment, namely, the wish not yet to have crossed, not yet to have entered the disappointment that is knowledge.

In light of the interpretation we are forwarding here, then, "typical dreams" such as that of being un- or underdressed in a public place acquire another layer of significance. Where else should the interpretation of such dreams lead us but to our earliest childhood experiences because it was at some point in the days of early childhood that jubilation in nakedness is replaced by the shame we learn to feel when naked in the eyes of strangers or even those well known to us? That the dreams of Freud's patients could only point us to memories dating from the middle of the nineteenth century provides delightful evidence for the utterly historical nature of the distinction between the naked and the dressed, as when one reports, "I was in my chemise or petticoat," or another, "I was walking in the street without my sabre and saw some officers coming up" (*ID* 276); for certainly nudity is a factor of cultural expectations that we internalize as part of our ethical fault-line, and the bedtime attire of the mid-nineteenth century would give little to dream about to generations accustomed to exposed backs, chests, midriffs, and legs. The affect provoked by such dreams can naturally vary from excitement to mortification because the subject experiencing this dream is testing the affective borders of his or her sense of shame. A practicing masochist or exhibitionist is nothing other than someone who experiences the enjoyment of this testing—along with that of the borders of disgust and pain—consciously as opposed to unconsciously. The typicality of dreams of nudity might ultimately lie in the aptitude of clothing as a metaphor for the very processes we are discussing. If "suppressed and forbidden wishes from childhood break through in the dream behind the exile's unobjectionable wishes which are capable of entering consciousness" (*ID* 280), can there be any doubt but that the unobjectionable wishes are an exterior that clothe and conceal an interior whose very value as interior, hidden, and objectionable is fully a function of that clothing, just as nudity is a function of the garb that simultaneously conceals and reveals it?

Our reflections now bring us to the troubled Oedipus and the controversial complex that bears his name. It can cause no wonder that Deleuze and Guattari's polemical treatise against the interpretive reductionism of psychoanalysis bears the title *Anti-Oedipus*. What doctrine reveals more perfectly that discourse's disdain for difference and multiple forms of desire than the one that states, "it is the fate of all of us, perhaps, to direct our first sexual impulses toward our mothers and our first hatred and our first murderous wish against our father" (*ID* 296)? What are we to make of Freud's reading of *Hamlet* as the story of a man who "is able to do anything—except take vengeance on the man who did away with his father and took that father's place with his mother, the man who shows him the repressed wishes of his own childhood realized" (*ID* 299)? Perhaps the first step is to mitigate our desire to read this within our traditional paradigm of interpretation, for Freud does not say (and following his own methodology *could* not say) that the real meaning of *Hamlet* is that Hamlet desires his mother and wishes to kill his father. As he puts it further on in the text, "just as all neurotic symptoms, and for that matter, dreams, are capable of being 'over-interpreted' and indeed need to be, if they are to be fully understood, so all genuine creative writings are the product of more than a single motive and more than a single impulse in the poet's mind, and are open to more than a single interpretation" (*ID* 299). Dreams and symptoms, it seems, need to be "over-interpreted" in order to be "fully understood," which would appear to be a patent contradiction if it were not for the fact that, in light of the understanding of interpretation presented in these pages, interpretation is not merely synonymous with understanding or a method leading toward understanding but is rather and much more an inherently excessive enterprise, one that always results in an over-interpretation because it consists in the translation between and among meaning systems or constellations, one of which alone would be enough for an understanding. Dreams and symptoms are "fully understood" only insofar as they have been allowed to be productive of an excessive interpretation and are therefore fully understood, or complete, only retrospectively in the moment we are, as it were, done with them—not so much because they are exhausted as because we have passed on to something else. If literary texts are somehow analogous, as Freud appears to be arguing, they also require a kind of excessive interpretation, such that an ultimate understanding lies helplessly beyond the horizon of at least one more interpretation.

As this defense of Freud's reading practices might seem nothing more than crafty and, well, defensive, I want to conclude this section with something that will be more recognizable as a productive misreading and something that will bring Oedipus in line with the arguments presented to date. Lacan's interpretation must form the basis of my reading because what Lacan saw in Freud's insistence on desire for the mother and hatred for the father was a particular cultural and familial instantiation of the incest taboo, a more specific rendering of taboo as such. Father and mother cease to be specific familial and gender relations and are rather understood as culturally specific manifestations of signifying relations: father standing in for prohibition and mother for that which is prohibited, eventually taking on the value of surplus enjoyment—in other words, whatever I might be enjoying that, for whatever reason, I am not enjoying now. Oedipus, in Lacan's rewriting, is the principal mythical rendering of a relation that would appear to be constitutive of being-symbolic; namely, prohibitions happen and we are thus always in relation to things prohibited. The fable's "lack," for which psychoanalysis is taken to task, is owed to the importance and centrality of this insight to its practice, but it seems to me that the irritation it provokes is misplaced: the "lack" so central to psychoanalysis has a similar status to the "not" that Freud at times would seem to banish from the unconscious and at times reinstate. "The way in which dreams treat the category of contraries is highly remarkable," he says. "It is simply disregarded. 'No' seems not to exist so far as dreams are concerned," a statement he promptly negates soon thereafter (*ID* 353, 361). Yet the reason for this ambivalence is easy to understand: as we have seen, and as is conveyed by the notion of condensation in the dream work, at each step along the way in the construction of dreams contrary thoughts are fused. That is to say, depending on the perspective of your reading, a dream thought can either carry a negation (reversals, contrary representations) or not (because the reversal simultaneously implies and conveys what is reversed). Lack, to carry this analogy to its conclusion, only appears as such from one side of a barrier, obstacle, or institution; institutionalization of any kind produces what we can call lack-effect, which taken from another perspective is merely the production of difference.

2

The Psychosis String

The psychosis string finds its origin in an autobiographical text published in 1903 by Daniel Paul Schreber, a powerful judge and political figure in turn-of-the-century Leipzig.[1] Freud apparently read this book during the summer of 1910 and discussed it at length with his friend Sandor Ferenczi while on a trip to Sicily that September.[2] The following year he published his *Psychoanalytische Bemerkungen über einen autobiographisch beschriebenen Fall von Paranoia (Dementia paranoids)* [*Psychoanalytic Observations on an Autobiographically Described Case of Paranoia*]. Lacan, who had developed an interest in psychosis as a student of psychiatry even before his turn to Freud and had written his doctoral thesis on paranoia, chose to devote the third year of his Paris seminar to a reading of Freud's reading, which he used to bring into greater relief his developing theory of the human subject's relation to language. Deleuze and Guattari have Freud's interpretation of Schreber's book in mind (along with many other texts) as they launch their attack on the institution of psychoanalysis in 1972 with the publication of their polemical manifesto *Anti-Oedipe*. These three interpretations compose the string under consideration in this chapter, in which I ultimately argue that some of the fundamental aspects of Deleuze and Guattari's critique of psychoanalysis in fact are already at work in Freud's original interpretation and elaborated on in Lacan's.

The Incommunicable World

One paradox of deconstruction can be phrased as follows: that which recommends deconstruction as the most rigorous possible philosophical discourse is that which drives it beyond the borders of comprehension. In other words, deconstruction takes the indeterminacy of signification so seriously as to refuse its own words, the words it uses to carry out its deconstructive operations, the stability necessary to achieve what traditional philosophy would recognize as understanding. This is why philosophy must refuse, or resist, deconstruction.[3] How could it not? The implicit backbone of philosophy, what could justify its claim in Kant's system as the queen of the sciences,[4] was its injunction to the production of "clear and distinct ideas," an injunction articulated by Descartes in his conversations with himself,[5] an injunction intended to help lead the searcher out of the murkiness that characterizes both self-knowledge and the language in which it is couched. If ideas are clear and distinct, then a particular idea or concept will have a determinate meaning, which will be expressible in terms of a predicated subject. Hegel first demonstrated with the kind of rigor that deconstruction has made its own that predicative logic must fail because it fails to grasp how the Notion (*Begriff*, "concept") functions. That Hegel uses *Begriff* can only mean that what he has in mind is the functioning of language, and he tells us as much.[6] Notional thought allows language to function as language does, in that it realizes that no subject can be predicated without in turn becoming another subject; predication invariably alters the subject of predication, requiring further predication, producing in turn further alteration. When philosophy grasps this, it can do so only at the cost of sacrificing the injunction to clarity and distinction that grounded its time-honored claims to truth: the very language that seeks to describe this motion is also subject to it.

For this reason deconstruction has always been something akin to a Deleuzian concept-producing machine. Derrida invents a term and uses it in full awareness that the term, insofar as it designates the very border of designation or signifies the border of signification, ceases almost at the moment of its minting to perform the function for which it was produced. *Différance*, the trace, the supplement, hymen, singularity, a seemingly endless list of terms that—although when read in the context of the specific arguments from which they emerge all, of course, do a specific work—are all also and at the same time, as Derrida says, the names of "what is possible only as impossible."[7] That is to say—and we say this because understanding can only be ultimately a function of translation and iteration—the names name the very impossibility of being named that allows other names and their meanings to take shape, but even that impossibility runs the risk of mistaking itself for something possible to communicate and hence misunderstand. Yet we are driven to run that risk and to rewrite, when we believe, as always occurs, that the misunderstanding has emerged in the form of a concept, of something formal and unchanging.

To try again, what is possible only as impossible might also be described, as Derrida elsewhere does, as that which gives rise to oppositions without partaking in an opposition itself or which produces distinctions without itself being distinct.[8] Of course, the moment we think it, we have imported a distinction into it and it is now a concept, predicated and predicable, and that original division again slips through our grasp—which is why we call it something else and try to protect it from other people's definitions and consequently from their understanding. It becomes sacred for us; or rather the sacred is nothing other than the culture-wide defense system built up against just this.

The invocation of a defense system is not alone in yet again reminding us of the proximity of deconstruction and psychoanalysis. Indeed, like any number of philosophical discourses and even discourses within deconstruction itself, it must be admitted that psychoanalytic thinkers fail continuously to break through their own resistances, to resist partaking in a culture-wide defense system such as that of ego-psychology, or perhaps even that of psychoanalysis in any doctrinal or institutionalized form. Lacan turned more and more to schemas and quasi-algebraic formulae, earning him ridicule from scientists and opprobrium from intellectuals, but one can understand the impulse. Derrida tried to focus our momentary attention, our ephemeral understanding, on the changeability underlying change itself by surreptitiously changing a letter, a vowel, in one word, a change imperceptible to speech and hearing, only recorded in writing and hence indicative of the unconscious generation of differences that necessarily precede our conscious distinctions. The letter he interposed was *a;* a little *a,* almost an object if we could grasp it in our hands and make it worth something, if we could make it speak in a pure way, letting us into its identity, *id-ens*, its being-to-self, without it always passing the buck to something else, as identity invariably does (*D* 132). If Derrida produced this letter, should we be surprised that Lacan produces his, somehow hoping that a letter, a symbol, a schema, will resist for a while the irresistible pull of signification and its distinction-generating machine? The desire is similar: it is the desire for a kind of "pure writing"[9] the impossibility of which both thinkers are perfectly aware, all the while being equally aware that its very impossibility is inscribed into everything their thought seeks to elucidate. As Derrida put it once in an interview:

JD: In my memory, what I write resembles a dotted-line drawing that would be circling around a book to be written in what I call for myself the "old new language," the most archaic and the most novel, therefore unheard-of, unreadable at present. This book would be completely different from the path that it nevertheless still resembles.
Q: Are you going to write it?
JD: You must be joking.[10]

Interestingly enough, the desire for such an old new language is manifested in a distinctly psychotic way—in that it emerges not as a desire for what one does not have but a reality out there in the world—in the delusions recorded by Senatspräsident Daniel Paul Schreber and analyzed by Freud. According to Schreber's paranoid theological system, "In the course of their purification souls learn the language which is spoken by God himself, the so-called 'root-language.' This is a 'vigorous though somewhat antiquated German, which is especially characterized by its great wealth of euphemisms.' "[11] What is most delightful and at the same time intriguing about Schreber's notion of a root-language is not merely that it be a version of the natural language he claims as his own. (Indeed, Judeo-Christian theology long held that Hebrew was the closest language to God's original intentions, to his very thoughts, so if God speaks any language he might as well speak yours, especially if you are paranoid.) What is even more remarkable is that this language, so close to God himself, would be characterized by its wealth of euphemisms, as if even God's own tongue is incapable of calling a spade a spade.

How are we to read this strange appearance of the euphemism, of a language that refuses to say what it means, at the very heart of a paranoid delusion—a structure whose purpose is to repair the rent at the heart of the world rather than reveal it because, as Freud says, "the delusion-formation, which we take to be a pathological product, is in reality an attempt at recovery, a process of reconstruction" (*TCH* 147)? The psychotic, Freud claims, is incapable of overcoming his resistances, but the resistances themselves are revealing because they make such a relatively feeble attempt to conform themselves to any popularly accepted vision of the world. In our implicit understanding of the world there is of course also a pure language, but if this language of God, whether it be Hebrew or some kind of concept-free mental telepathy, is lacking anything, it is certainly lacking euphemisms, metaphors, and anything else that might interfere with the direct transmission of intention. In the psychotic's world, in contrast, there is nothing but euphemisms all the way down.

The reason for this is that in his rupture with the communicable world—a pretty good working definition of psychosis—the psychotic has been forced to confront something that nonpsychotics in their socially acceptable delusion have never been confronted with, or at least are well protected from by the nature of our social defense systems: the psychotic has touched bottom in language and knows there is no bottom there. He has experienced full force the trauma of deconstruction and has come back to tell about it, but of course his language no longer makes any sense. The truth deconstruction tells is traumatic,[12] but it is so in and toward an institutional context; when it gives up on rigor it becomes poetry, also institutionally recognized, and when it maintains its rigor it is caught up in a dialect of miscomprehension and neologic production. Were one to comprehend deconstruction, really comprehend it without engaging in the translation/concept production that has become its modus operandi, one would in essence be psychotic too. Perhaps our greatest thinkers, like our greatest poets, as well as all those world-historical figures who were not recognized in their time, walk that line in a perilous way.

What distinguishes Schreber from a poet or philosopher is, of course, that he self-identifies as a psychotic, that he comes out and admits that he really believes the delusion he is describing. Upon reflection, is this delusion so much wackier than the one a good number of Christians will tell you is literally true and would die for, or the one a good number of Muslims will tell you is literally true and would die for? Where does this distinction lie? The answer consists of two aspects: first, Schreber inhabits his own private delusion[13] because his psychotic episode ruptured his bonds to other, publicly sanctioned delusions; second, Schreber's delusion reveals certain radical truths, integral to his rupture with the world, which it is the business of culture-wide delusions to avoid at any cost.

We have already seen in the case of the *Interpretation of Dreams* how Freud's method involved, as he puts it in this text, stripping "his sentence of its negative form, to take his example as being the actual thing, or his quotation or gloss as being the original source" (*TCH* 110)—that is, a technique aimed at regressing through a history of change enabled by the poetic tropes available to language. The dream, as we were told, enacts the opening and closing of the unconscious much as a transferential situation does[14] but does so moreover in the form of a having-been-experienced that is remembered or reconstructed as such in the moment of the awakening. The psychotic state, for reasons we will now venture into, allows for the same unconscious regression without the intervention of the loss of consciousness, awakening, and subsequent memory event associated with dreaming. What the dreamer remembers and reconstructs, the psychotic experiences *tout court*.

Let us recall the paradox of de-liberation that is operative in dream experience: reflective, de-liberative thought re-presents the dream thoughts in such a way that they have been experienced as presented and hence liberated from the constraints of rational, communicative thought while at the same time again de-liberated in that the dreamer is enslaved by experience; his or her impressions are (were) incorrigible. The liberation from de-liberation is akin to a letting down of the guard of consciousness and is a state that can be aroused by weariness, by drugs, or willfully in the psychoanalytic setting, with the result that for a limited time that conscious agency of distancing and reflecting is diminished. In the psychotic state, the liberation of the unconscious apparently occurs without necessitating the lessening of conscious oversight, which means that the consciousness is faced with not only the constant input of perceptions from reality but also the constant input of what would otherwise be unconscious statements— which might have found their way into consciousness as dreams that had been experienced—in the form of conscious, waking experience. The psychotic actually lives Hegel's assertion that thought and existence are identical

(Hegel, *Phenomenology* 490) but does so without the counterbalance of an external communication community whose implicit function is to set a standard for what is conscious and communicable and what is to be sloughed off and hence unconscious. The psychotic, in other words, inhabits in a fully conscious way both sides of his ethical fault-line.

Freud's thesis concerning the etiology of paranoid psychosis is that the sufferers "attempt to master an unconsciously reinforced current of homosexuality" and in so doing come to grief (*TCH* 136). This homosexual current, in accordance with Freud's consistent de-pathologization of homosexuality, is not to be understood as diseased or abnormal; nevertheless, there is a notion of developmental abnormality in his theory: manifest homosexual desire in adults is a throwback to a stage of previous development, before the ego learned to cathect objects or the other with its libido. Narcissistic attachment to the ego as object is in this view a natural stage in the development of the ego and should by all rights be followed by a detachment from the ego and re-investment in an object. "People who are manifest homosexuals in late life have," Freud goes on to say, "never emancipated themselves from the binding condition that the object of their choice must possess genitals like their own" (*TCH* 137). Putting aside Freud's controversial etiology of homosexuality (for he was not beyond believing that homosexuality needed an etiology), what is of interest here is to read this attempt in conjunction with the regressive theory that is also at the heart of the *Interpretation of Dreams* and that he forwards again toward the end of this case history.

Here Freud outlines a three-step theory of repression: the first step, fixation, consists of the assertion that "[o]ne instinct or instinctual component fails to accompany the rest along the anticipated normal path of development, and, in consequence of this inhibition in its development, it is left behind at a more infantile stage. The libidinal current in question then behaves in regard to the later psychological structures as though it belonged to the system of the unconscious, as though it were repressed" (*TCH* 143). If we understand drive as being always in relation to a particular institutionalization, then it becomes clear that the "normal path of development" cannot be read as a natural path but is rather one determined by "anticipations," which must be conceived of as socially normative.[15] A drive that has been left behind in such a way is only conceivable in relation to and as the result of a process of institutionalization that already includes—in the form of, for example, anticipations—future or "later psychological structures." A fixation, in other words, not only lays the groundwork for repression ("The second phase of repression is that of repression proper"); it is at the same time the result of repression and its very content. Thus, the repressed or fixated drives are remainders of "infantile stages" and are always at the heart of what we desire, although what we desire, and here's the rub, has to undergo a kind of baptism in the marketplace of values, for we will ultimately desire what is sanctioned as being desirable by a community with which we identify. If and when such a community is not formed or a particular drive is in such conflict with that community as not to be capable of producing a desire (here an example would be the manifestation of homosexual desire in an ego that has literally no place for it), then the repression can be of a kind that outstrips the normal dialectic of the unconscious, *depriving it of the very community that banishes it to invisibility and yet provides it with the fabric of its existence.* Such repression, which Lacan will call foreclosure,[16] dissolves community as such and simultaneously short-circuits the very distinctions between thought and perception that give our sense of reality its consistency.

Let us examine more closely the theory of regression as it is outlined in this study of psychosis. The psychotic patient is understood to have some portion of his libido fixated at an earlier, narcissistic or just post-narcissistic and hence homosexual stage of object choice. This fixated libido is repressed by the remaining, normally developed psychological structure because its manifestation would be unacceptable to the conditions of social acceptability inherent in the secondary processes. The conditions for pathological development would thus seem to be two: the particular nature of the fixation must be sufficiently different from "the rest of us," for as we have already noted drive functions via a series of fixations and repressions; and the relation between the fixation and the rest of the psychological structure must be incommensurate enough that the subject's only remaining line of action is radically to withdraw his libido from investment in the world per se. It is this choice that would seem to determine psychosis in opposition to other pathological manifestations, and it is for this reason that we see in Schreber's delusional reconstruction a step whose role is to account for this total withdrawal of libido, or interest: "The end of the world is the projection of this internal catastrophe; for his subjective world has come to an end since he has withdrawn his love from it.

(Note: He has perhaps withdrawn from it not only his libidinal cathexis, but his interest in general—that is the cathexes that proceed from his ego as well)" (*TCH* 146). It is of interest that here and a little later in the text Freud entertains and indeed does not reject the notion that libido should not be restricted to some notion of sexual energy (*TCH* 150). In agreement with the notion of drive or drivenness I have argued for here and elsewhere,[17] the investment of libido becomes a simile for interest per se, for investment, being-toward-the-world and being-toward-others. It is also of interest that in the *mise en scène* of its delusion the psychotic ego reproduces *ad extremis* what could be called the fundamental fantasy of the metaphysical world view, or at least its logical vanishing point, in the paradox of solipsism. The paranoid's "conviction that the world has come to an end and that he alone has survived" (*TCH* 150), or even more trenchant, that the people around him are nothing but contraptions created for the sake of maintaining him in a deluded state, what are these but versions of the idealistic conviction, pilloried by Hegel, that the world is but a projection of the all-powerful I?[18] That this thesis would seem to flow naturally from the very form in which the problem of epistemology presents itself— that is, how do I know that what I sense is true?—is mirrored in the ease with which the paranoiac can rationalize his convictions with the fact of perceiving otherwise: "I can no longer avoid recognizing that, *externally considered,* everything is as it used to be. *Whether, nevertheless, there may not have been a profound internal change* is a question to which I shall recur later" (*TCH* 145). Certainly, the infallibility of this remittance to the fundamental independence of internal and external reality in justifying any particular narrative or constellation of meaning cannot appear strange to us because it is at the core of practically every belief system in existence, systems whose function is to "save appearances" while maintaining a core narrative in the face of whatever evidence to the contrary. One can only admire the ingenuity of the psychotic along with that of the devout creationist, for whom the "scientific fact" that fossil evidence dates life to millions of years ago does nothing to undermine the fact that God created the world as it is a mere 5,000 years ago because the fossils and their apparent age are simply part of God's creation. The difference again is that in the latter case the believer is not alone in his or her delusion.

What is the point of this digression into a comparison between paranoid strategies and the philosophical discourse of modernity, unless it is to

suggest the existence of some kind of affinity between the two, a suggestion that would bring us into dialogue with Deleuze and Guattari's thesis
concerning the relation of schizophrenia and modernity? To grasp the rapprochement, especially in the face of these thinkers' fundamentally critical
attitude toward Freud, we need to overlook for a moment the fact that
Freud's etiology focuses on the role of the father as an individual in Schreber's particular psychological structure and look rather at the distinction
he draws between paranoia and dementia praecox or schizophrenia. For
Freud, the two conditions share fundamentally the same root cause, namely,
"detachment of the libido, together with its regression onto the ego"
(*TCH* 152). The fundamental difference lies in the point of fixation, that
of schizophrenia occupying an even more primordial stage of development than that of paranoia, resulting in a prognosis that is "on the whole
more unfavorable than in paranoia" because "[r]egression travels back not
merely to the stage of narcissism . . . but to a complete abandonment of
object-love and to a restoration of infantile autoeroticism." In another formulation, in the case of schizophrenia "the victory lies with the forces of
repression and not, as in the former [paranoia], with those of reconstruction" (*TCH* 153).

Modernity, as I have argued elsewhere, is best characterized not by
the emergence of the so-called modern subject or by any particular kind of
subjectivity; rather, what consistently distinguishes the modern from the
late medieval world is its predominant spatiality, which I have called theatrical. In theatrical spatiality the principal metaphor for understanding
one's self in its relation to the world and others is as an actor playing a
character in front of an audience, which is in turn composed of characters
being played by actors.[19] If the particular forms of psychosis have a historical character and moreover one visible in the philosophical discourse of
modernity, then the following analogy would seem justified. Whereas the
paranoiac instantiates the extreme of a theatrical subject model in which
the subject deals with the revelation that he or she is nothing but a character by reinforcing that character according to a delusion of megalomania
or by consciously *realizing* the presence of an audience that non-psychotic
subjects experience implicitly, the schizophrenic instantiates the opposite
extreme of the very same model: either totally refusing to act (catatonia) or
giving up on any structuration whatsoever to his or her self-presentation.
World and self and perception and unconscious thought are all equally and

at the same time options for perception and action; *the divisions constitut-ing the modern world are rejected at the very same time as they continue to de-termine the nature of that reaction*, for there can be no doubt that the very pathology of the schizoid subject is a symptom of that world, the world it outlines at one extreme with paranoia guarding the other.

The parallels with Deleuze and Guattari are thus clear: there are two extremes of reaction or directionality possible within the socioeconomic framework provided by capitalist modernity: fascism, an essentially para-noid reconstruction of lost reality around the figure of a leader, and schizo-phrenia, the anarchistic tendency to follow "lines of flight" down toward their extremities; to embrace molecular structures that dissolve molar ag-gregates; to remain at the edge of and engage in the production of bodies without organs, bodies like that of Schreber's, "who lived for a long time without a stomach, without intestines, almost without lungs, with a torn esophagus, without a bladder, and with shattered ribs[;] he used some-times to swallow part of his larynx with his food" (*TCH* 92).

If we follow this line of thought, what we see is that Schreber was a schizoid subject who was more or less successfully reconstructed in a para-noid vein; indeed, part of Deleuze and Guattari's critique is that Freud and psychoanalysis collaborate at least implicitly in that reconstruction. If we consider that in his own, more strictly philosophical works Deleuze has dedicated himself to rescuing certain thinkers from their incorporation into the hegemonic current of modern philosophical discourse—a current dominated by the epistemological conundrums of mind-body dualism—reading them in such a way as to stress their resistance to that current or the alternate models they propose, then it may not come as a surprise to see aspects of such "schizophrenic" systems emerging in Schreber's delu-sions. For instance, in his theological system, we find a human being whose psyche and soma are inextricably intertwined to the point of nondiscern-ability (at times, although the paranoid fantasy of soul death comes in to shut this line of flight down). "The human soul is contained in the *nerves* of the body. These are to be conceived of as structures of extraordinary fineness, comparable to the finest thread. Some of these nerves are de-signed only for the reception of sensory impressions, while others (the nerves of understanding) carry out all the functions of the mind; and in this con-nection it is to be noticed that each single nerve of understanding represents a person's nature and mental individuality" (*TCH* 97), an assertion that cannot fail to recall Leibniz's definition of his monad as expressing the whole of the universe, as well as Deleuze's salvaging of Leibniz for his counter-narrative to modern philosophy.[20]

In the logic of such a physio-theology—in which God consists of nothing but nerves, capable of "turning themselves into every imaginable object in the world" (*TCH* 97)—the fundamental distinctions of external-internal and appearance-essence that structure the delusion run their course or follow their lines of flight in the opposite direction, into a mish-mash in which body and soul and human and God become ultimately indistinguishable. The irruption of the unconscious, then, is clearly structured along certain institutional demarcations, or fault-lines, from the eschatological to the scatological—hence, "The need for evacuation, like all else that has to do with my body, is evoked miraculously" (*TCH* 101), in the form of God's mischievous suggestion, "Why don't you sh——?," at the same time that He always makes sure to send someone else to the lavatory at just the right moment to prevent the satisfaction of that impulse. This centrality of the fault-line is the principal explanation for why at the center of Schreber's world the question of sexual difference is to be found writ large.

"One morning," Freud reports, "while he was in a state between sleeping and waking, the idea occurred to him 'that after all it really must be very nice to be a woman submitting to the act of copulation'" (*TCH* 88). The most important step in Freud's interpretation of this case, in fact, is his insistence on placing priority on this aspect as opposed to leaving it as expressed in the patient's self-analysis, that is, as a secondary condition of his function as redeemer. Although he does not draw out the consequences in so many words, Freud's point is that the redeemer fantasy is the megalomaniacal reconstruction of an ego torn apart by a wish, which itself represents a schizoid reaction to the particular institutionalization of sexual difference. The voices that say to him, "So this sets up to be a Senatspräsident, this person who lets himself be f——d!?" (*TCH* 95), are nothing if not the very real voices of social opprobrium whose purpose is to ensure the inviolability of one of the fundamental distinctions underlying all meaning systems. The symbol of the border distinguishing men and women, dividing their desires, identifications, and reproductive functions, for example, is the phallus, which is psychoanalytic language for that which gives rise to oppositions without partaking in an opposition itself and which sexuated language tries invariably to situate within the field of differences and hence to determine. "Phallus" in all rights should be (and I think this is the correct reading of its Lacanian manifestations) positioned along with that list of deconstructive signifiers that try to name that which is only possible as impossible. If such an incorporation is resisted, it is because psychoanalysis insists that the problem of sexual difference is somehow more fundamental than other differences—that it is somehow distinguished among differences by precisely its universality, one it shares with language and hence with deconstruction itself. Yet does the designation of the phallus do a service by recognizing a problem that is real or a disservice by reinforcing and universalizing socially determined differences?[21] Arguments on both sides are compelling, but what Juliet Mitchell remarked years ago, that to know the devil is not equivalent to doing his work, still seems right to me.[22]

The Exclusion of the Other

How do we situate our thinking about the nature of interpretation within the analytic discussion of the psychoses? Lacan brings the two issues into a direct dialogue when he states, "The irreducible elementary phenomenon [of psychosis] here is at the level of interpretation" (*III* 20). In order to better grasp this, we need to return to a distinction regarding the mechanism of psychosis theorized by Freud, namely, that between *Verdrängung* and *Verwerfung*. "When I speak of his having rejected [*verworfen*] it, the first meaning of the phrase is that he would have nothing to do with it in the sense of having repressed [*verdrängt*] it" (*TCH* 12, trans. modified), Freud writes in his Wolfman case study, and the emphasis latent in the notion of repression, here negated, is that repressing something is quite clearly having something to do with it. As Lacan glosses, "repression and the return of the repressed are just the two sides of the same coin. The repressed is always there, expressed in a perfectly articulate manner in symptoms and a host of other phenomena. By contrast, what falls under the effect of *Verwerfung* has a completely different destiny" (*III* 12; see also 46).

Let us not fail to note the extraordinary power this distinction has held and continues to hold in contemporary philosophy. Indeed, the notion of abjection that comes to us from Kristeva's work, Irigaray's thinking about the place that women do not have in language, and even Butler's insistence—in the context of her critique of Irigaray—on that dimension of beings who are refused the sort of social articulation that would entail existing at all: all of these imply a dialectic that opens up a further negation beyond negation itself. For if negation is precisely a move that situates the negated in relation to something affirmed and therefore grants it a kind of secondary existence, then these discourses all posit the notion of some thing that exceeds or is extruded from even this process, that thing[23] on whose fundamental exclusion the very distinctions of sociality are founded.

We are under no obligation to take the familiarity of this concept as evidence for its truth. Let us rather merely acknowledge that it plays a functional role in the psychoanalytic understanding of the psychoses and go forward from there. Recall that the notion of repression with which we are working—as illustrated by Lacan's allusion to the metaphor of the coin—refuses the traditional topographical gesture of indicating some place beyond the ken of consciousness. What is at stake, rather, is a logical process deriving from the intrinsic ambiguity of signification, or "The Antithetical Meaning of Our Primary Words,"[24] in Freud's own words— and here I would add "even" before "our primary," stressing the clear and overwhelming ambiguity of so-called higher or abstract terms. In this process, the flow of signifiers that constitute thought as such, in coming to conform to the constraints of a communicable understanding, shed a continual series of negated but nevertheless possible options for signification. The line that would be produced by hypothetically connecting the dots of this series of negated possibilities would constitute at the same time repression and the unconscious, or the very drive to recuperate these possibilities would constitute that unacceptable desire or drive that is the unconscious.

One cannot logically pursue all of these tributaries of thought once one has been baptized into the communities of communication in which we are represented by our understanding. This is the definition of impossibility, and that it is impossible constitutes the meaning of castration. Impossibility is, however, itself traumatic and must be represented within the world of understanding, which it is via the signifier of negation. Prohibition replaces impossibility, and in this way a place is made for castration that has the consequence of saving face for the ego: "You cannot because you must not! (But if you were permitted, you probably could . . .)." Our understanding of psychosis must therefore take place against the normative backdrop of neurotic desire, and against this backdrop Lacan tells us that "it can happen that a subject refuses access to his symbolic world to something that he has nevertheless experienced, which in this case is nothing other than the threat of castration" (*III* 12). What I would suggest in the service of clarification is that the threat in question is precisely that the prohibition is not necessary, that it is not merely the constraint of authority that keeps us from enjoying our unconscious desire; rather, desire itself is impossible.

The template of "normal," neurotic desire, then, is that what is repressed from the symbolic will return in the symbolic. This return can take the form of neurotic symptoms or, as we have seen, the fairly benign form of dreaming in which the symbolic is experienced via the imaginary, all the while maintaining the very flexibility and ambiguity that characterize it as symbolic, an order in which "every element has value through being opposed to another" (*III* 9). In contrast, the psychotic undergoes something quite other than repression, something in which "whatever is refused in the symbolic order, in the sense of *Verwerfung*, reappears in the real" (*III* 13); in other words, as hallucination.

The fact that hallucination is described here in terms of the return of the foreclosed in the real may be at first glance a source of confusion. It would appear that the correct interpretation of hallucination according to Lacanian theory would be that what is foreclosed returns in the imaginary, for is it not the imaginary that comprises the world of sense perception? Although the realm of the senses is indeed that of the imaginary, to conceive of it as that exclusively would be to commit the error of conceiving of the human being as being in a pure, unadulterated, or unmediated relation to perceived reality. Insofar as the subject is always already a subject of symbolic mediation, the tripartite categorization can be read as follows: the real is the level of material perception; the imaginary is the level of determinate meanings, that is, that of perceived reality according to the order of the understanding; and the symbolic is the level of the system of exchange and reversibility that enables the unconscious.[25]

In one sense, then, what we claim about psychotic experience is— and here we return to Lacan's claim that the fundamental elements are at the level of interpretation—that the psychotic interprets what pertains to the symbolic in terms of the imaginary: "Everything has become a sign for him" (*III* 9), or, as he puts it later, "the world has begun to take on a meaning" (*III* 21). But does not the world already have meaning? What, then, is so specific about the psychotic interpretation? This, however, is precisely what is *not* the case in normative psychical functioning: because meaning is always in reference to some other meaning, there will by definition always remain an element in a formulation that is entirely devoid of meaning, radically indeterminate. In the expressions "everything has become a sign" and "the world has begun to take on meaning," we see that the totality has been granted a meaning and has been rendered in that sense determinate. This is why Lacan insists on the notion of the understanding or realm of the understandable: in psychosis, what in principle cannot be understood is situated at the level of understanding (*III* 21).

If we say, therefore, that the psychotic interprets what pertains to the symbolic in terms of the imaginary, then what we mean is that he or she translates the former, with all of its flexibility and reversibility, directly into perceived reality. To put it another way, the psychotic's discourse, a discourse of words, is necessarily symbolic, but the raw material of that discourse "is his own body," the relation to which is "the restricted, but really irreducible, field of the imaginary" (*III* 11). If the field of the imaginary is to be thought of as irreducible (hence not subject to the production of meaning as referral to further meaning) and as "always at the limit of the symbolic" (*III* 11), we begin to grasp that the imaginary register gains its value in the Lacanian theory as the border or touching between the flexibility of the symbolic and the absolute, material unknown that would be the netherworld of perception—unknowable because knowledge itself can only be a function of faculties restricted to "this side" of that border. Is this not, then, a version of Kantian schematism? For Kant the imagination (*Einbildungskraft*) is "an effect of the understanding on sensibility" and has the function of synthesizing the manifold of intuitions of the sensible world;[26] in Lacan the imaginary marks the same border and cannot be conceived of independently of its imbrication with the symbolic order as marking the very limits of the articulable. When words fail, we turn to an image; an image arises where signification ceases. One way or another, the image is determinate in relation to a network of signifiers; its relative stability accounts for what we might call the stability of our sense of reality.

It is because the psychotic's reality retains precisely that stability that we do not speak of the return of that which has been foreclosed in the imaginary but rather in the real. For the source of those voices, those signs, and those evil intentions is perceived in exactly the way the voices, signs, and intentions that impinge on non-psychotic imaginaries are perceived. Like any symbolic element and unlike an imaginary one, a judgment on a delusion is entirely context dependent; "take them [descriptions of delusions] out of context and you will see the most wonderful descriptions of the behavior of everyone. It was touch and go whether what I read out loud from Kraepelin's definition of paranoia defined normal behavior" (*III* 19). The delusion, unlike the stabilized reality of the imaginary, is a structure, but one whose elements are imaginary. Now we can venture an explanation for why although the psychotic interprets the symbolic at the level of the imaginary what is refused from the symbolic returns in the real. For the psychotic the symbolic has taken on what could be called the rigidity of the imaginary.

At the level of the signifier the psychotic is driven to produce neologisms out of a nagging suspicion concerning the word's slipperiness;[27] at the level of the signified the psychotic's delusion is characterized by the fact that "the meaning of these words can't be exhausted by reference to another meaning. . . . It's a meaning that essentially refers to nothing but itself, that remains irreducible" (*III* 33). These two levels correspond in turn to two forms of reception of the word, the intuition, in which the word is full, "overflowing, inundating" and the formula, in which the word "no longer refers to anything at all." These "two forms, the fullest and the emptiest, bring the meaning to a halt[;] it's the lead in the net, in the network, of the subject's discourse—a structural characteristic in which, once we approach it clinically, we recognize the mark of delusion" (*III* 33). This rigidity, in which the normal flow of meaning has been brought to a halt, means that for the psychotic, the symbolic has been for functional purposes elided out of existence; some other register must take up the role of signification in relation to the imaginary-symbolic block, and that dimension is the real.

If this aspect of the psychotic mechanism has been clarified, then we have still not touched upon the etiology of *Verwerfung*. What is it about this refusal of something in the symbolic that instigates the sort of structure we have been calling psychotic? According to Lacan, this aspect of the mechanism is founded in speech, *parole*, insofar as it is to be distinguished in the idiom of structural linguistics from language, or *langue*. The point of his invocation is to align this distinction with the one explored above between the imaginary and the symbolic, in that speech is to the imaginary as language is to the symbolic, or speech acts as the same kind of point of stoppage to the infinite reversibility of language as the imaginary does for the symbolic. Just as the relatively stabile reality of determinate imaginary meanings exists always as a reference point for or epiphenomenon of the unconscious world of possibilities of the symbolic, so does the determinate instantiation of speech exist or signify only in relation to the radical indeterminacy of language. This is what Lacan means when he speaks of speech as testimony or bearing witness: "Precisely what constitutes the foundational value of this speech is that what is aimed at in the message, as well as what is apparent in the feint, is that the other is there as absolute Other. Absolute, that is to say that he is recognized but that he isn't known. Similarly, what constitutes the feint is that ultimately you do not know whether it's feint or not" (*III* 38). In other words, when speech takes place, for example, between two people, part of what is at stake is the bearing witness to the absoluteness of the Other, something akin to the perfect knowledge or transparency which we theorized as the fundamental presupposition of communication. Even if I cannot make my thoughts clear, the presumption is that they refer to something that could be flawlessly transmitted and that the Other who can transmit that thought is out there, "beyond that reality [in which my speech is now taking place]" (*III* 51).

At this point we must recognize a strange reciprocality or at least interchangeability to the positions we have ascribed; for if language, in the form of the Other, is instituted by the practice of speech as an indispensable beyond, then it is no less the case that the system of rules, the game of exchanges that is language, depends on a "beyond" that is a contingent and momentary act of speech, a committing or establishing of someone in the position of implicitly recognizing the speaker: "This speech is therefore always beyond language. And such a commitment, like any other utterance, even a lie, conditions all the discourse that follows, and here, what I understand by discourse includes acts, steps, the contortions of puppets, yourselves included, caught up in the game. Beginning with an utterance a game is instituted" (*III* 51). The Other, then, relies for its existence as guarantor of speech on a point of fixation beyond language, a contingent act of naming, for example. Speech, in its radical contingency, relies for its role in communication, identity formation, and so on, on the "beyond" of that absolute other instituted by the very moment of its utterance. It is this Other, as should be clear by now, that has been excised, removed, refused, in the triggering of psychosis.

That the ego is already in some sense other for the subject, in that it is first an object in the world, subject to the recognition of another for its own unity and consistency, determines "within the speech relationship, something that originates somewhere else—this is exactly the distinction between the imaginary and the real. A primitive otherness is included in the object, insofar as primitively it's the object of rivalry and competition" (*III* 39). The rivalry and competition emerge from the imaginary relation insofar as that relation contains and presupposes the something other that is the very definition of the real. This aggressivity, as Lacan calls it in his essay of that title,[28] is the foundation of paranoid knowledge, a knowledge that is only "overcome in speech insofar as this involves a third party" (*III* 39). It is the implicit witness speech bears in its very utterance to a being outside of the imaginary relation—outside its particularity and evanescence but also outside its fixity—it is the very fiction of an index of universality, in other words, that holds the paranoid knowledge, that is, delusion, at bay: "In delusional speech the Other is truly excluded, there is no truth behind, there is so little truth that the subject places none there himself, and in the face of this phenomenon, this ultimately raw phenomenon, his attitude is one of perplexity" (*III* 53).

How is the Other excluded? Lacan cites Jean Hyppolite's intervention on the concept of negation in the seminar of two years previous, in which he argued that "behind the process of verbalization there must be admitted a primordial *Bejahung*" (*III* 12). It is perhaps not too much of a stretch to link the primordiality of this yeah-saying to the primitiveness of the otherness inscribed in the ego as first object and further to the utter contingency of those first speech acts—not the ones that mark a subject's entry into language, for they can only be retroactively posited as such long after the fact, but those whose utterance marks the onset of a game, committing the subject to a position within a symbolic structure. By bearing witness to an absolute Other in his or her speech, in his or her act of commitment, a subject surreptitiously acknowledges the otherness at his own heart; by thus bearing witness with his contingent utterance, he implicitly grants the groundlessness of his being and hands his hopeless hope for meaning over to the Other. It is this primitive utterance that constitutes the primordial *Bejahung* prior to verbalization and this the *Bejahung* that the psychotic subject refuses to admit. The result of this refusal is a psychic reality that "itself initially contains a hole that the world of fantasy will subsequently fill" (*III* 45).

But why, to reiterate, this refusal to admit? To this I can only submit that "the something different" in the psychotic's history is that in it the subject has, as I put it before, touched bottom only to find that there is no bottom there. The horror of that encounter is too much for the psyche to bear, and in place of a primordial admission there is silence.

Reality and Uncertainty

In the course of his lectures on the psychoses, Lacan distinguishes between reality and certainty in the context of his claim that psychosis has fundamentally to do with the level of certainty rather than with that of reality. This distinction provides the basis for an interpretation of Lacan's interpretation of Freud—and in this case of the case study of the "madman Schreber"—that situates Lacan's thought squarely outside the boundaries of a representationalist world view, precisely at that time, relatively early in his career, when his thought seems to be most impregnated with precisely such a model. As I noted before, there are times when Lacan's schemas would seem to borrow directly from the sort of conceptual scheme that tends to be associated with the high metaphysics of Kant insofar as they presupposed a division of the world according to the restrictions of knowledge over against the unknowable world.[29] One of the ramifications of addressing this issue is, at least implicitly, to raise again the question of the relation between psychoanalysis and philosophy and to broach that pretension that would make psychoanalysis precisely that queen of the sciences that philosophy failed to be in its descent from Kantian metaphysics to the analysis of plain language. That we might find clues to this relation in an exploration of the psychoses can be explained only by the notion in Lacan's study that in psychosis what is fundamentally at stake—and in a way surpassing that of normative subjectivity or the neuroses—is the subject's relation to language.

That psychoanalysis might qualify in some sense as the queen of the sciences is not to be taken as a methodological manifesto for a kind

of sociological approach to knowledge via the psychoanalysis of the prac-
titioners of science. The simplest defense possible to any perceived en-
croachment on science's claims to truth from its situatedness in a
sociological study is that such situatedness, precisely because of its universality, can never be understood as inherently altering our evaluation of a
practice's conclusions. Whatever Einstein's feelings for his father might
have been alters nothing about the reliability of his theories concerning
space, time, and gravity. Similarly, Freud's theories concerning human behavior and desire answer to the standard of a kind of symbolic reproduction or reproducibility, which could serve as a general theoretical model
encompassing truth criteria as disparate as experimental reproducibility in
the physical sciences to the spread and growth of religious doctrine: what
is true is what works, and the meaning of the word *truth* alters according
to its use in specific contexts or disciplines.

This said, the only possible meaning for the notion of psychoanalysis as queen is that the realm of its basic concerns incorporates all others,
perhaps in the same way the philosophy of everyday language purports to
but in the case of psychoanalysis without objectifying language use or, in
other words, turning Dasein into something present-at-hand, an object
among others in the world. Psychoanalysis incorporates philosophy in that
it in-corporates it, embodies it, treats philosophy as discourse and its insights as being fundamentally about the nature of embodied discourse.
This is why psychoanalytic thinking,[30] like Heideggerian thinking, is not
often concerned (or should not be) with disproving other discourses but
rather with thinking what Heidegger called the Same,[31] that is, considering what possibly it is about human experience that could have led someone to say just that.

Let us take an example from the lectures on the psychoses. In rapid
succession Lacan cites Aristotle, Descartes, Einstein, and the Judeo-Christian
tradition on the notion of deception:

> Take Aristotle. Everything he says is perfectly communicable, and neverthe-
> less the position of the nondeceptive element is essentially different for him and
> for us. . . .
>
> Well, whatever minds satisfied with appearances—which is often the case
> with free-thinkers, and even the most positivist among you, indeed the most lib-
> erated from any religious idea—might think, the simple fact that you live at this

precise moment in the evolution of human thought does not exonerate you from what was openly and rigorously formulated in Descartes's meditation about God as incapable of deceiving us.

This is so true that so lucid a personality as Einstein, when it was a matter of handling that symbolic order that was his, recalled it—*God,* he said, *is clever, but he is honest. . . .*

It need hardly be said that matter does not cheat, that it has no intention of crushing our intentions or blowing up our machines. This sometimes happens, but only when we have made a mistake. It's out of the question that it, matter, should deceive us. This step is not at all obvious. Nothing less than the Judeo-Christian tradition was required for it to be taken with such assurance. (*III* 64–65)

The point about matter's inability to deceive can be taken even more to heart now that the quantum revolution has produced that monument to saving appearances called the Standard Model, because the very purpose and function of the Standard Model is to demonstrate the reliability of predictions at the inconceivable levels of energy and minuteness at which matter is revealed to be fundamentally deceptive.[32] Even where matter deceives us, we might then add, the law does not or must not, which keeps physicists focused on such goals as quantum gravity and other GUTs and TOEs (grand unified theories and theories of everything). Lacan's point, of course, is to reveal within this sampling from 2,000 years of intellectual history that "The dialectical correlate of the basic structure which makes of the speech of subject to subject speech that may deceive is that there is also something that does not deceive" (*III* 64). The difference between Aristotle and the latter examples is the difference of the Judeo-Christian break: whereas Aristotle was assured by visible nature of "the truthfulness of the Other," it was "the radicality of Judeo-Christian thought on this point that made possible this decisive step, for which the expression act of faith is not out of place, which consists in supposing that there is something absolutely nondeceptive" (*III* 65).

The point of convergence between these discourses, like that of the discourses discussed earlier, is at what Lacan calls the level of certainty rather than that of reality. Certainty, regardless of our propensity to classify it along with fact over and against such failures of certainty as mere opinion, is a function of belief. Certainty is belief that has been distinguished by the believer as no longer being stained by the uncertainty haunting the rest of his or her own beliefs or the beliefs of those others that he or she happens not to share. Belief, along with its subcategory certainty, is a symbolic affaire. Belief and certainty are independent of the experience we would call that of reality. Let us take as an example a classic debate in analytic philosophy. You pick up the most recent *New York Review of Books* and read an article in which you discover that it has been conclusively demonstrated that Shakespeare was not the author of his plays but that an unknown playwright from Stratford called Humbert Humbert was. Immediately we realize that this discovery depends very much on certain choices of articulation. Do we now say Shakespeare did not write his plays, Humbert Humbert did? Do we rather say the man we have known as William Shakespeare was really Humbert Humbert? Does Humbert Humbert cease to be primarily the name of a character from Nabokov and become the new name for the author formerly known as Shakespeare? After initial confusion, our collective decision would eventually emerge out of argumentation and subsequent discoveries. Further historical information about a real person named Will Shakespeare who did not write the plays but received credit for them would lead to one naming practice, whereas the discovery that there was never such a person as William Shakespeare but only Humbert Humbert would lead to another. After all, we call George Eliot and Sting by their *noms de plumes*.

The lesson to be gleaned from these examples is that our knowledge concerning, for example, the authorship of Shakespeare's plays is a knowledge situated, like all knowledge, in the field of belief and certainty and moreover stretched between the two like a line between two poles. The articulation of the knowledge of the authorship of these plays is a matter of certainty—as certain, for the time being, as the knowledge of what makes a light bulb glow—because it approaches the aprioristic density of tautology, insofar as Shakespeare is little more (unless you are a Shakespeare biographer) than the name we give to the one who wrote those plays. At the moment this certainty is shifted toward the pole of belief by a new articulation (Humbert Humbert wrote Shakespeare's plays), the belief that was certain is treated as deceptive over against another, stop-gap certainty (someone wrote those plays) until the new certainty can be reestablished (Shakespeare was the pen name of a guy named Humbert Humbert, but we'll continue to call him Shakespeare for old times' sake).[33]

The point of certainty, then, functions as a kind of pivot around which discourse can turn, beliefs can be discussed, and knowledge can be formulated and exchanged. Such points of certainty are legion, and strangely enough, as we have just seen, individual points can apparently change without causing much disruption. When Lacan insists that psychosis concerns fundamentally the level of certainty rather than that of reality, what he wishes to emphasize is that whereas in relations of knowledge characterized as normal the point of certainty is utterly independent of imaginary impressions—they tend to be definitions, tautologies, laws, principles—for the psychotic the "world . . . is transformed into what we call a phantasmagoria, but which for him has the utmost certainty in his lived experience. This is the game of deception that he maintains, not with another like himself, but with this primary being, the very guarantor of the real" (*III* 69). As we can begin to see, Lacan interprets Schreber's delusion as a map of the psychotic relation; it is a psychotic symptom, but it also and at the same time represents in the imaginary the structure of psychosis as such. It represents exactly what it is, or it collapses the difference between being and representation, just as the psychosis collapses the difference between the imaginary and the symbolic. To put it another way, Lacan reads Schreber's delusion as a kind of dream rebus whose dream thought is the limit-situation or breakdown of the symbolic relation that sustains normative subjectivity. This is how Lacan explains the peculiar personality of God in Schreber's delusion: "Ultimately God's greatest danger is to love Schreber . . . too much" (*III* 69). To love him too much would mean precisely to be "caught at his own game"; that is, God has been dragged away from the point of absolute distance and neutrality, the stability that guarantees the real, and into the imaginary relation with all its aggression and eroticism. "But the pivot of these phenomena is the law, which here lies entirely within the imaginary dimension" (*III* 69–70), Lacan says, and it is thus in the imaginary, or reality, that is played out the drama of deception and certainty that functions so fluidly when confined to the symbolic—but which, in the context of said reality, provokes the outbreak we call psychosis.

Let us look at how Lacan expresses this phenomenon, which he calls the elementary phenomenon of psychosis, and which he says must be situated at the level of interpretation: "Reality isn't at issue for him, certainty is. Even when he expresses himself along the lines of saying that what he experiences is not of the order of reality, this does not affect his certainty that it concerns him. This certainty is radical" (*III* 75). It seems then that

st such radical certainty to what would be in the case of the
ct "a state of blissful uncertainty" because for such a sub-
the rarest thing," and "if he questions himself about this
be aware that certainty emerges in strict correlation to an
action he undertakes" (*III* 74). For normative subjectivity, then, such radical certainty is unusual, and when it occurs it tends to be the correlate of
an action such that the action in question crystallizes a certain perspective
on the world or collapses a set or series of alternative potentialities for action into one, the certain one. For that subject what is not an issue is precisely the certainty of that stabilizing point from which the meaning of
reality is guaranteed; it is implied but not at stake, and the steady transmission of knowledge called communication takes place largely with disregard to certainty. For the non-normative subject the stakes are different,
as he or she demonstrates a radical intolerance for such uncertainty, for
what we could call the indifference of reality. For such a subject everything
regards him or her, and whether or not impressions may be real is utterly
irrelevant to that fundamental regard.

This is, it seems to me, how we are to make sense of Lacan's distinction between the madman and the poet, in which the latter corresponds to
one whose "writing introduces us to a world other than our own and also
makes it become our own, making present a being, a certain fundamental
relationship" (*III* 78) whereas the former fails to present in his writing anything with "the feeling of an original experience, in which the subject is
himself included—his testimony can be said to be truly objectified" (*III*
77–78). A poet, in other words, bears witness to the uncertainty at the vanishing point of knowledge precisely by writing in the space between possible subject positions, by presenting a self not as object of certainty but as
subject of ultimate uncertainty. The psychotic, in contrast, has no way to
speak of himself other than as an object, an insight that Schreber's map of
psychosis presents as well in the form of a God who can only have knowledge of cadavers.

The implicit point of certainty, which simultaneously allows normative subjects to inhabit a state of blissful uncertainty concerning all matters
large and small, this vanishing point and guarantor of knowledge gives the
normative subject a great deal of room for the satisfaction of drives that
are, after all, oriented along the very fault-lines of symbolic uncertainty.
We can locate such fault-lines at work already in Freud in his notion, for

example, of the great polarities of mental life. There is no lack of clarity as far as Freud's definitions of masculinity and femininity are concerned; they are simply the cultural masks of a more fundamental psychical opposition between the active and the passive. Although the attribution can no doubt serve as ample fodder for feminist critiques of Freud, it is crucial to note the liberating impulse of such a designation, which refuses to grant any psychical content at all on the basis of sexual identity but rather locates a culture's assignment of such identity in a kind of misconstrual. There is no eternal masculine and feminine; society has merely portioned these roles out according to its understanding of truly universal dichotomies, dichotomies owing their consistency to a certain quality of the signifier to raise at the moment of its utterance the specter of its negation. This means that the assumption of active models of identification in accordance with a masculine ideal implies the existence of drives oriented along the faultline corresponding to such assumptions and hence toward the adoption of so-called feminine forms of enjoyment. A subject whose knowledge is liberated (to a certain extent) from lived uncertainty by the implicit certainty of a nondeceptive symbolic pivot may satisfy such drives through a variety of means—condensation, repression, and negation all being ways of speaking of the negated or elided desire. But Schreber, Lacan says, "never integrated any feminine form" (*III* 85), as is evident from the nature of his delusion.

The integration of a feminine form, that is, of a form negated by one of the primary institutionalizations of identity formation for a man, takes place in normative male subjects according to the above-mentioned functions, all of which are made possible by the Oedipus complex, the fact that "the ambiguity and the gap in the imaginary relation require something that maintains a relation, a function, and a distance" (*III* 96). That Schreber's delusion tends to act out in a literal fashion the very mechanism of his pathology means for Lacan that God's failure to keep his distance, his very entry into a competitive and erotic relation with Schreber, is an illustration of the failure of the Oedipus complex. This failure resonates profoundly at the level of primary institutionalization, insofar as "in order for the human being to be able to establish the most natural of relations, that between male and female, a third party has to intervene"—which itself puts the lie to the naturalness of such relation in humans—"one that is the image of something successful, the model of some harmony." Patriarchy's self-conception might fit here, and this would be the meaning of the phallus, but "This does not go far enough—there has to be a law, a chain, a symbolic order, the intervention . . . of the father. Not the natural father, but what is called the father. The order that prevents the collision and explosion of the situation as a whole is founded on the existence of the name of the father" (*III* 96). It is quite well understood that the father is a function in Lacan's thought, normatively filled within the heterosexual matrix by a biological father but in principle independent of this social identity. Here, however, the definition of that function becomes quite refined: whatever third term interrupts and hence prevents the internal collapse of imaginary relations, that is, whatever term serves the function of guarding access to that being that would be the ultimate guarantor of truth, this term in its symbolic manifestation is the word of the father. Thus both fundamental aspects of the failure of the Oedipus complex are patent in Schreber's delusion: the loss of the father function becomes a God who is unable to maintain his distance, his independence, and Schreber's transsexuality becomes the ultimate replacement, in the imaginary, of the impossibility that function sustains and makes tolerable—the impossibility, namely, of a harmonious relation with the other.

Psychosis and Interpretation

Let us recall our definition or redefinition of interpretation in the opening chapter, in which we stipulated that, as opposed to a traditional notion that would have the practice of interpretation be primarily involved with unearthing a meaning lying hidden behind an obfuscating wall of signifiers or as being somehow more original in respect to a history of secondary or parasitical transformations, the notion of interpretation with which we are concerned conceives of meaning as the very result of those transformations and as inconceivable outside a relation that would precisely emphasize such a radical mobility and fungibility. Rather than attributing meaning to an original intention, for example, we conceive of meaning as being the shuttling between positions of intention and reception or being nothing other than the very force of attribution itself.[34]

At this point the discourses of psychoanalysis and philosophy merge or emerge around the pivot of this redefinition, for if we rethink meaning in to this light, then the unconscious must equally be rethought out of its topographical mold as a place of hidden meanings and into a new form, one highlighting that the meaning of the unconscious must be sought in the shuttling movement of meaning per se. If we take from Heidegger the suggestion that Dasein is the being that questions itself about its own being, then we find that the being it is questioning itself about is the very meaning of the unconscious, a bipolar logos within Dasein or of which Dasein can be said to be. To clarify the relation to Heidegger, if the latter defined in his own idiom Dasein as a play of closure and disclosure—as opposed to the traditional view of a subject being in a representational relation to a world of beings—then the unconscious, in our new idiom, becomes the name for the very shifting border of that play.

The unconscious is the constitutive interpretation of a being whose being is a question for itself but whose self-questioning and hence interpretation are a disturbance or threat to its socially established existence. Indeed, interpretation in this light is threatening because it would appear to undermine stability or rationality (one reason for every event, every decision), because it would seem to say to the ego, *you are not the entity that you say you are; your values and beliefs are not grounded in the way you would like them to be.* But this threat is also what psychoanalysis calls castration, and in our redefinition or interpretation of terms we suggested that the threat of castration is nothing other than the possibility the subject senses that prohibition is in some sense futile, that the impossibility of the fulfillment of desire—a desire oriented along the arabesque traces of infinitely bifurcating tributaries of thought—is constitutive and not contingent upon the capricious prohibition of one in power. The ego is built around this protective "no" like a pearl around a grain of sand; the ego becomes a gem stone about which one forgets that its original purpose was to protect us from something quite irritating: interpretation.

(Of course you will see that a sort of ambiguity has crept into my discourse, for interpretation is an irritant, but it is also the balm, the sheen of the pearl, as it were, that protects us from this irritant. It is characterized by a double movement, which we will explore.)

Wo es war soll ich werden,[35] said Freud, and *soll,* I suggested at the outset of this discussion, needs to be read in the sense of an ethical imperative but not perhaps as we tend to understand an ethical imperative. It is not that the "I ought to" becomes itself in the place where the id was but rather that the becoming of the ego on the traces of the id (or the traces that comprise what we call the id) marks a border or line that is the very place of the ethical itself. Ought, obligation, the sense of duty, emerges in the very same place that desire does or that drivenness per se does, that is, on the border between the institution of the ego and the dissolution of interpretation. This is how I have defined the ethical fault-line,[36] the line that *marks* fault as undesirable and at the same time *spurs*[37] the desire to pursue it right through to the demise of the ego and its entire moral framework. That such desires are not consciously articulated, that at some level there remain always desires that cannot be consciously articulated, is the meaning of repression.

This structure arises already from a reading of Freud's earliest work, for in the *Interpretation of Dreams* what we are confronted with is a theory concerning the relation of concepts and images in which the deliberative work of the concept removes the one who has dreamt from the liberating (because undirected by deliberative thought) and simultaneously capturing (because sensory experience has the quality of incorrigibility) realm of the imaginary, lifts him or her out, and creates a certain distance. This deliberative distance is both a liberation from the flow of dream thoughts as experience and another kind of enslavement, a subjection to the strictures of meaningful communication, of reason, of understanding, and of morality. In the terms of Lacan's schematic thought, the distancing of de-liberation is the work of the Other, the other place of language, the guarantor of certainty that allows for deception and truth to play off one another. It is, as we will discuss further on, the very structure of the Oedipus complex, and the force of its appeal is the threat of castration, the threat that prohibition is futile. Insofar as Oedipus—or the acceptance of the external signifier, the distance of de-liberation—allows the subject to avoid imaginary capture, it functions as a kind of interpretation. What else is this level of interpretation but the establishment of a deliberative distance from that interpretation, that shifting and moving along with the flow of concepts that is the imaginary? The crucial difference is that it is only this distance that allows the imaginary to flow as it does, for without it the imaginary becomes rigid, locked into immobile patterns of quasi-instinctual experience.

The passage to a new reality is what I called the awakening. It is in the awakening that the subject, called forth to speak and hence deliberate on his or her experience, distances himself or herself from that experience, makes it experience in contrast to the narrative that positions it in time as pastness, that resolves the virtuality of that flow into that which was experienced. This experience, however, will only ever have been in the passing moment of the awakening, the fleeting moment of present deliberation of the experience as experience, itself drifting into pastness in the very moment of its enunciation. The awakening is the call to a decision in the realm of certainty, a decision that frames an imaginary reality as that which was experienced. This framing and the distancing that enables it comprise our experience of time: the emergence of a present out of virtualities that only exist as such from the perspective of their retrospective resolution into a lived experience, or a dream, for the structure is analogous. It has been a source of constant fascination for me to observe the emergence of a time consciousness in my children. *Gestern* ("yesterday"), they say, and will proceed to give word to something that either just happened or perhaps happened last week or last month, an experience that is realized (in its etymological sense) as experience in the very moment of its being situated within a general frame of pastness, which in the relatively less cluttered mind of a two-and-a-half-year-old is released by the single signifier *gestern*.

The subject of the awakening is difficult to grasp, and it seems indispensable to turn to literature, which can have the distinct advantage of displaying imaginatively ideas that are difficult to formulate in the direct fashion of linear discourse. To digress only slightly, I would argue that one of the most fruitful interpretive borders is precisely that between literature and a writing about literature that could configure itself as criticism or theory or philosophy insofar as in any of these discourses what is ultimately at stake is an attempt to make something explicit, although by doing so one runs the risk, even necessitates it, of losing something else that has an essential relation with remaining implicit. Perhaps literariness might be redefined as that which remains implicit after each attempt to make the meaning of a text explicit, a redefinition that would position the literary at the very source of meaning or align it with the border between disclosure and closure that marks Dasein's bipolar logos, its unconscious.

The text to turn to here is one we have already mentioned in passing as a text about dreaming, awakening, and what happens that might provoke one into failing to make the distinction. *Life Is a Dream*, says the title of Calderón's most famous play, a morality piece about how a prince, and a man, learns to tame his wild nature and become civilized. Fearing the starry signs' prediction that his son would grow up to kill and replace him, like Oedipus, Polish King Basilio has him locked up in a tower from birth, where his jail keeper Clotaldo is his only communicant. Utterly confined, utterly powerless, Segismundo is offered no rationalization for his suffering and no one to take responsibility for it either. Bitten by remorse, Basilio decides to test the prophecies, by now somewhat self-fulfilling, by releasing his son on a kind of probation. He will be drugged and then will awaken from his sleep in a palace surrounded by servants and sumptuousness; he will be told that this was always so, that he has awakened from a long and troubling dream. The backup plan will be that should he show his nature to be violent or contrary at any time, he can be drugged again and replaced into his tower, and the brief time out of prison will be revealed to have been the real dream.

This is, of course, exactly what happens, and after killing an attendant and attempting to rape the heroine, Segismundo is returned to captivity and all is explained to have been a dream. The similarities to what Lacan says about psychosis are remarkable:

> Let's suppose that this situation entails for the subject the impossibility of assuming the realization of the signifier father at the symbolic level. What's he left with? He's left with the image of the image the paternal function is reduced to. It's an image which isn't inscribed in any triangular dialectic, but whose function as model, as specular alienation, nevertheless gives the subject a fastening point and enables him to apprehend himself on the imaginary plane.

> If the captivating image is without limits, if the character in question manifests himself simply in the order of strength and not in that of the pact, then a relation of rivalry, aggressiveness, fear, etc. appear. (*III* 205)

If we can assume that for Segismundo the realization of the signifier "father" is impossible at the symbolic level—because what such a symbolic realization would entail is precisely a prohibition, a name, a genealogy, something that places him within the order of things in a way that justifies his existence or at least in a way that keeps its non-justifiability from erupting into plain view—if this realization has become impossible, then Segismundo's aggression can be explained according to the theoretical model Lacan presents. Segismundo orients himself toward the world in general along the model of his pure rivalry with his father, an unadulterated, unmitigated fight for power and the right to enjoy.[38]

What is fascinating for our purposes is the way that in Calderón's play this regression into the imaginary register goes hand in hand with a loosening or even complete dissolution of the distinction between reality and the dream world, which is to say between the deliberative distance that frames imaginary realities and categorizes them according to pastness, or in relation to a certain index of certainty, and those imaginary realities themselves. There is from our perspective no dream that ever takes place in *Life Is a Dream*; nevertheless, the dream motif or that of the possibility that the reality being experienced may turn out to be a dream at the moment of the awakening determines the entire moral tenor of the play. What Segismundo eventually learns is something akin to the integration of a fundamental signifier, for example, the signifier *father*, into his symbolic order, and the way he learns it is to fear the threat of castration, namely, to fear that the reality he is inhabiting may be nothing more than a dream and that the enjoyment it furnishes may disappear in smoke at the time of a future awakening. Insofar as one fears this eventuality, one relativizes one's experiences against some future point of certainty, hitherto unrevealed, which yet creates that distancing, that spacing inherent to symbolic mediation. By believing that life may be a dream, one ceases to live life as a dream and lives it rather as reality, a world that has already succumbed to some form of negation, a world that is therefore not constantly running the risk of the immediate dissolution of its own omnipotence. This reality resolves itself as such precisely in respect of what Lacan would call a "blissful uncertainty," namely, uncertainty as to which of an infinite range of virtualities we might be choosing at the moment to recollect, call our own, call our past, or call our dreams. By learning this, Segismundo can become a man, become a king, return to the world of the living.

Let us pause to schematize. We have theorized the existence of two levels of interpretation. For the time being we will adopt a Freudian taxonomy and call them primary and secondary interpretation. Primary interpretation is the realm of creativity, of what we could call the symbolo-imaginary, in that in it, and like the dream work, the subject follows the paths of thought laid down by the movements of the signifier; out of its virtualities something called reality is resolved, but dreams are too, as are visions and literature. Nevertheless, the work of this symbolo-imaginary would not take place; it would in fact never resolve as such or have the freedom to move in the ways it does were there not a second level of interpretation, that which we have called de-liberation but which also goes by the names of distancing, communicability, and even Oedipus. The example of Segismundo illustrates that this level of interpretation depends on the integration of a signifier that is oriented around a paternal function insofar as that function fits one into an order but at the same time holds imaginary reality at bay and by so doing creates it *as reality*, as something that could be lost were it all only a dream. Insofar as one identifies with a name, one's identification with and immersion in lived experience are mitigated, and it is this mitigation that allows for something called reality to separate itself off from the virtuality of an unlimited imagination. By not making that move of identifying with a signifier that is in itself without justification, the subject risks psychosis, the foreclosure of symbolic identification and the symbolic order as such that leads to the inability to resolve an imaginary reality that one can relativize from the standpoint of some communicable language. By failing to accept the uncertainty of life (life may be a dream), life becomes a dream.

The mistake to avoid, then, is the one that is all too often the assumption in critiques of Lacanian thought, namely, that the phallic function and the paternal function are the same. Where the phallus is truly at stake is in the relation between the mother and child in which, Lacan says, "a mother's requirement is to equip herself with an imaginary phallus" and "As to the child . . . whether male or female it locates the phallus very early on and, we're told, generously grants it to the mother" (*III* 319). But, he goes on to say, this harmonious couple, mother and child, is not permitted to continue in "this common illusion of reciprocal phallicization. . . . because, the phallus is, as it were, a wonderer" (*III* 319). If we can say that the father's function in the trio "is to represent the vehicle, the holder, of the phallus," then what this means is that from the perspective of the supposed interrupted harmony of mother and child the father has what they do not or is the very reason for their not having it. What is crucial, however, is to recognize that the purpose of the paternal function is to be "that which in the imaginary dialectic must exist in order for the phallus to be something other than a meteor" (*III* 319).

What is a meteor? In its original usage, *meteor* [μετέωρο] denoted an atmospheric appearance of inexplicable origins; it was a *phenomenon*, as Lacan says. Coming from the Greek for raised, lofty, even sublime, the meteor signified that above which there was nothing else or, as Lacan says, "nothing is hidden behind it" (*III* 318). If something appears in the imaginary with nothing hidden behind it, no meaning to refer to, no explanation to situate it, then it functions as a kind of stop-gap. Reality is filled, lived as experienced, not subject to any relativizing perspective; it is just this: an ultimate phenomenon, a meteor. Were the phallus (that which the child wants, that which the mother wants) not to be attributed to someone else (the paternal function), then it would act as such a stop-gap; it would hide nothing behind it; there would be no uncertainty, but there would still be words, and these words, whose relationship to lived reality is normally secured, would emerge in this subject "through the accompaniment of a constant commentary on his gestures and acts" (*III* 307). "Phallus," then, is no more than the final element in a chain of associations. The question is, does it stop there, fully justified, or does it point somewhere else, somewhere I cannot fathom but that some one, some figure has knowledge of? Our certainty of the latter, a certainty that allows us to negotiate reality in a state of blissful uncertainty as to its fundamental meaning, is what keeps us at the minimum distance from experience needed for it to be resolved into reality, to be reported on, communicated about, disagreed over. What we should keep in mind, however, is that while the refusal of symbolic quilting can indeed lead to the total isolation of psychosis, the primary interpretation that is the substance of that world is also our only hope for freedom, personality, creativity, and even philosophy in this other world. Where we are left is with secondary interpretation, with its potential uses and abuses, which are of course the subject of *Anti-Oedipus*.

To Space or Not to Space

I ended the previous section by stating outright that the stakes in Deleuze and Guattari's critique of psychoanalysis concerned the level of what we have been calling secondary interpretation, the institution of a minimal distance between the subject and his or her imaginary reality. Such a minimal distance or spacing is the requisite condition for there to be such a thing as reality in the first place because it is instrumental in the sort of framing function that allows an imaginary plenum to coalesce into a field perceived as coherent and as somehow entailing an existence that is independent of the subject. If Deleuze and Guattari can be read as situating their critique at the level of secondary interpretation, this can be understood in a number of ways. On the one hand, such a critique could be understood as radical, meaning that what Deleuze and Guattari find at fault is secondary interpretation per se insofar as a secondary interpretation would entail a necessarily constraining of and ultimately damaging incursion into the multiplicity of forms that desire can assume. On the other hand, the critique could be understood as selective, meaning that what is at stake is the kind of secondary interpretation that is either implicitly or explicitly condoned by psychoanalytic theory and practice. If the first reading is accurate, then we should expect to find in their work and in Deleuze's philosophy as a whole a radical rejection of the kind of minimal distancing I have described; if the second reading is to be preferred, then we will expect to find throughout their work examples of such spacing, and the possibility will remain for some kind of productive dialogue between psycho- and schizoanalysis.[39]

Although it is out of the question to attempt to survey the entirety of Deleuze's thought in this brief space, it nevertheless makes sense to hone in on the critiques in *Anti-Oedipus* and *A Thousand Plateaus* from the perspective of a broader understanding of Deleuzian thought. To this end, one can begin by stipulating certain equivalences between Deleuzian concepts and those of other fields of thought, with the knowledge that upon honing in certain differences (which will turn out to be important, if not fundamental) may emerge. Yet on the basis of this process what one perceives is not the futility of the older concept but its transformation, its susceptibility to what I have called interpretation, albeit not in the form ridiculed by Deleuze and Guattari as "interpretosis."[40]

To begin with, we will stipulate a general equivalence between what psychoanalysis has called the unconscious and what Deleuze and Guattari call the plane of imminence. In *What Is Philosophy?* they define the plane of immanence as being "presupposed not in a way that one concept may refer to others but in a way that concepts themselves refer to a non-conceptual understanding."[41] If the philosophy articulated in a given temporal and cultural moment may be isolated as a plane, it "institutes a plane" that consists of the presuppositions of its conditions, and its "image of thought will be quite varied depending on the place that philosophy presupposes as its condition" (Lambert 6). Classical philosophy, for instance, situated this plane at the level of the representation of the idea, modern philosophy as the common sense responsible for apprehending the world, and perhaps contemporary philosophy as the sum total of other discursive or mediated forms through which knowledge is generated. As Gregg Lambert puts it, "to a greater and greater degree, contemporary philosophy poses its own ground in what is 'other than consciousness,' or what stubbornly remains outside the powers of representation, whether this is defined as the subject of the Unconscious (Freud), as the subject of a virtual linguistic structure (Saussure and Hjemslev) or of the 'Being of Language' as such (Heidegger), as a determinate moment within the economic sphere of production (Marx), the series or Markov chain in modern biology, or, more recently, in terms of the brain that is just beginning to be discovered by neurophysiology" (Lambert 6–7). Of course in Lambert's series the unconscious occupies only one point in the chain, a specific manifestation of the plane of immanence of modernity's image of its own thought, for Deleuze's realm is that of philosophy, which tries to think the plane of immanence "transcendentally," or in its totality (as opposed to "transcendently," or as an object to be referred to).[42] It is therefore to be expected that the other discourses will be situated within the overall field of "non-conceptual understanding" that it is philosophy's task to try to think. Nevertheless, if we think of the unconscious as a concept in Deleuze's sense, as a creative tool rather than something representing some other thing out there in the world or in our minds, then we maintain its potential to participate in an overall project of philosophy. What I like about Lambert's series is the way it too establishes equivalences and is thereby willing to think what Heidegger called "the Same" in the service of a new thought or toward the thinking of the plane of immanence. We should not forget that in the very midst of their critique of psychoanalytic methodology and presuppositions Deleuze and Guattari also proclaim that "the great discovery of psychoanalysis was that of the production of desire, of the productions of the unconscious," a discovery which was only later "buried under a new brand of idealism," namely, Oedipus.[43]

If the unconscious is good, then, it is good insofar as it functions as a plane of immanence, as God or Nature in the Spinozian universe, out of which the other various planes of expression emerge like so many tendrils or extensions of one substance. It does not lie behind conscious ideas as their unconscious meaning but is rather the very force of their production, and (a revised or renewed) psychoanalysis would become the practice of the exploration of this expressionism, or what we have been calling interpretation, in a similar way to how philosophy, in *What Is Philosophy?*, becomes "nothing less than a diagram of the brain (*le cerveau*) that is traced from the limits of sensibility to the conditions of thought, '*du dehors au dedans*,' attempting to discover in the perceived a resemblance not as much to the object of thought but rather to the force that causes us to think: the condition of sensibility and no longer the representation of its sense" (Lambert 5). Not only can Deleuze and Spinoza be glimpsed within this framework, but Heidegger and Freud and Lacan also begin to come into focus, for in all cases what is at stake in analysis (psychoanalysis, analytic of Dasein, schizoanalysis) is not the revelation of the truth about an object of thought but rather the discovery of what we could call with Heidegger the field of referentiality, or with Freud and Lacan the unconscious, or with Deleuze the plane of immanence, and specifically the discovery of how a particular image of thought emerges from that plane. Indeed, what has our careful reading of the *Interpretation of Dreams* revealed if not that the interpretive method is focused precisely on what can be called "the force that causes us to think"? This is why in the work of all three thinkers non-philosophical objects and discourses acquire such prominence: art, literature, and media practices are all fundamental aspects of how, in Heidegger's words, the world worlds.[44]

Before we get into Oedipus and the critique of secondary interpretation, it is worthwhile to return to the model we have been developing, on the basis of a careful reading of psychoanalytic texts, of how certain imaginary constellations coalesce into something we can call reality. The crucial point to grasp is that this model is in radical opposition to any notion of truth that might be described as conforming to the metaphysical presuppositions of a theory of correspondence. While it is easy to trump correspondence theories with the observation that ultimately sentences and the things they are supposed to correspond to are of entirely different natures and hence any correspondence is inescapably conventional and thus consensual, more sophisticated defenders of such theories are the first to grant that truth statements always have to take place within conventional frameworks. Nevertheless, they insist, the reality to which these statements refer exists prior to and independently of such statements, and hence the truth value of the statements must ultimately be measured in relation to that pre-existing state of affairs. Furthermore, there are many and even infinite events or states of affairs that must be said to exist despite a universal lack of knowledge of them or despite ultimately false conclusions about them, even if we assume these conclusions or this ignorance to be eternal. For example, although no one can or ever will know for sure how many, you have blinked your eyes an exact number of times in the course of your life, and that number exists regardless of our lack of knowledge of it. Or, to take a favorite example of Daniel Dennett's (although he too uses it to argue against correspondence theories), there would exist some geographical center in the universe to all the socks he has lost in his life. The existence of this "Dennett lost sock central" is utterly independent of any knowledge we or others may have or not have of it.[45]

What is wrong with all of these examples or, better, what these commonsensical examples reveal that is wrong at the heart of all correspondence theories of truth, is that by an almost imperceptible sleight of hand they pass off as imaginary what are in fact symbolic statements. There is, as they will say, an exact number of times you have blinked your eyes in your life, and a truth statement about this fact would present us with a number corresponding to that number. However, in the moment of invoking the example what they fail to acknowledge is that the correspondence they are seeking and are asking you to accept is not between a number and a number, a symbolic equivalence that we would have no problems accepting, but rather between a symbol and an exact imaginary scenario in which you "see yourself" blinking over the period of your life. Such a scenario not only will be irreconcilably different for each speaker, it also probably will be irreconcilably different every time it is invoked even in the same person, and hence the idea that there is a correspondence between a symbolic utterance and such a scenario is ultimately false. Such a truly corresponding sentence would have to catalogue the exact times of each blink, milliseconds or nanoseconds between them, the exact shade of blue worn by the waiter who asked exactly that question in exactly that way in that café in that city at the very moment, and so on. In short, it would have to be a sentence in the language dreamt of by Ireneo Funes, in Borges's story "Funes the Memorious," whose absolute memory made him intolerant of any generality whatsoever: "Locke, in the seventeenth century, postulated (and dismissed) an impossible language in which each individual thing, each stone, each bird, and each branch would have its own name; Funes once began a project for a similar language, but ended up rejecting it as too general, too ambiguous."[46] All of this is not merely to set the bar impossibly high for correspondence but rather to claim that the imaginary scenario that is slipped in as the ultimate reference for a corresponding truth statement is in fact already a symbolic selection; insofar as it is capable of correspondence, it is already articulable as a statement. It is only imaginary precisely to the extent that it exceeds such articulation and hence exceeds the possibility of correspondence.

This fact is expressed with cosmological significance if we take the example of Dennett's sock central to its logical extreme: given that the Earth spins around its axis at around a thousand kilometers an hour, that it moves through space relative to the sun at far greater speeds, that the solar system revolves around the center of the galaxy at unimaginable speeds, and so on, it becomes clear that the notion of a center in space and time of all of those objects called socks lost by an earthling over the course of the earthling's life is not only imaginary in the Lacanian sense but also imaginary in the colloquial sense. This notion requires a perspective on the universe that not only exceeds human capability but also is per se impossible. There is no such point because time and space, the very fabric of the imaginary, are not inert backdrops to our movements through the universe but constitute the very movement of the universe itself.[47] Yet it is precisely such imaginary impossibilities that constitute the implicit presuppositions behind our notions of truth. As Claire Colebrook succinctly puts it, "From the complex flow of time we produce ordered wholes—such as the notion of the human self. *We then imagine that this self preceded or grounded the flow of time rather than being an effect of time*" (Colebrook 41; emphasis in original).

Recall that in discussing the coalescence of the imaginary in relation to a point of uninhabited certainty—the coalescence constituting a reality that we can somehow relate to, call our own, and yet simultaneously be distant enough from so as to report on it and have disagreements as to its basic interpretations—we established that in psychoanalytic theory this process depended on the relation to an other. This other, however, could not merely be that other who fits so well into imaginary relations, my immediate other, my mirror image, and so forth, but had rather to be an Other in its essential unfathomability, an Other whose function is precisely to be unfathomable, unjustifiable, unknowable. The incorporation into my psychical world of this absolutely certain point of absolute uncertainty is what *spaces* my relation to an imaginary ensemble and allows it to coalesce. The moment of coalescence, structurally akin to the awakening at work in the production of dream worlds, determines a particular reality as real over and against a series of virtualities that only take on their patina of deprivation in that moment, as merely dreamed, merely wished for, merely possible. In a similar way the past emerges as such in that moment, as does the future, and time receives its recognized structuration. What is essential to grasp is that in the lived moment that which will become past is contained in and inseparable from that which will become present, and hence time cannot be thought of as a past-present-future spectrum along which the human moves as if moving from one place to another but rather and more fundamentally as the very production and generation of worlds that include images called pastness along with others called possibilities or possible worlds. One of the profound insights of Deleuze's *Bergsonism* is precisely its overturning of the traditional relation between possibility and reality, which held possibility only to be a lesser, superceded, shadowy form of reality. What Deleuze appreciates in Bergson's thought is the idea that "there is not *less*, but *more* in the idea of nonbeing than that of being, in disorder than in order, in the possible than in the real."[48] As he cites Bergson, "the possible is only the real with the addition of an act of mind that throws its image back into the past once it has been enacted" (*B* 17). It is this act of mind, then, that is at stake. Certainly (from a philosophical perspective) we are justified in insisting on the recapture of possibility, on the restitution of its place of privilege as a fundamental constituent of reality, and we can, as I have tried to show, come to this position from a reading of psychoanalysis as well as of Bergson or Deleuze (indeed, reality for Freud is also quite clearly a deprivation of possibilities, the work of the secondary processes, that intervenes in hallucinatory satisfaction, for example). Nevertheless, the status of this act of mind remains in question, and it is to this that we will now turn our attention.

It can come as no surprise, given our discussion to this point, that among Deleuze's favorite philosophers can be counted Leibniz, the German thinker and mathematician who theorized that our world could only have been selected by God from an infinite number of other possible worlds. The nature of an event that marks the emergence of a possible world dominates Deleuze's thought from an early stage, emerging from his ruminations on

Bergson to take a prominent position in his first work of philosophy not explicitly dedicated to another thinker, *Difference and Repetition:* "*What Happened?* In other words, what causes the past to become 'the past'? *What is going to happen?* 'What are the conditions of an event that causes the future to become 'the future?' "[49] The conditions of the event in question are clearly another variation on Bergson's act of mind that structures time as we recognize it. As Lambert says, "the fundamental problem of judgment concerns the nature of a certain decision that determines the conditions of any possible world. But what does it mean to 'decide?' " (Lambert 20). For Deleuze, one possible answer to this question would be the Cartesian answer, in which the thinker doubts, thereby distances, and casts the world into a particular thought image, that of the *cogito* as guarantor of the relation between thought and world or being. What Leibniz does differently, among other things, is to make the act of decision a kind of infinitely suspended one in which we inhabit the world that we do precisely because God selected it, and God, as the absolute manifestation of rationality and hence reality could only have selected *this* world out of the infinite other possibilities.[50] As a graduate student at Stanford in the mid-1990s, I invited Andre Linde to speak at an interdisciplinary conference on time about the controversial multiple universe theory with which his name is largely associated. He came across as a colorful figure with great computer visuals of what he liked to call the "Kandinsky universe," but one had the impression his Nobel laureate colleagues also regarded him as colorful and his theories as mere speculative flights of fancy. It is therefore all the more striking that he should now be at the forefront of science legitimate enough to count itself among the news that's fit to print, as one of the foremost proponents of a model of the universe or universes that could have been written by Leibniz.[51]

The problem at the heart of current debates is the so-called anthropic principle, the idea that the universe is designed to support life. The notion was coined by Brandon Carter, who in 1974 argued that in the face of the evidence that the various constants at work in the universe would have had to be "set" within a hair's breadth of what they actually are set at in order to ensure the possibility of any life whatever, it nevertheless should not surprise us that they are so because research into nature is not likely to discover laws that would exclude our existence.[52] The strong version of this principle has been expressed by Freeman Dyson as the idea that "the universe must have known we were coming," a formulation that led string theorist and Nobel laureate Steven Weinberg to call the principle "little more than mystical mumbo jumbo."[53] Against the notion of a universe predisposed for life, string theorists seek to describe one based on an elegant and ultimately simple set of formulae to explain all physical laws in the universe. What string theorists hope to prove, for example, is that there are sound mathematical reasons for why the "dials of the universe" are set as they are, for why the weak gravitational force is what it is, or for why the mass of certain fundamental particles is what it is. If we put this debate in the perspective of the Leibnizian model, however, it is the string theorists who would seem to be courting the more anthropic of the two models because by denying that "God has a choice" in what universe to preserve, which laws to favor, they are in essence arguing that the laws of mathematics dictate a world built to our specifications and that no other world is possible. Multiple universe theorists, on the other hand, can be read simply as saying that we are in our universe and not in another because this one happens to be one in which the conditions for life emerged, a formulation in which the decision of God has turned out to be nothing more radical than the observation that one always seems to find what one is seeking in the last place one looks.

It is also not surprising that proponents of the standard model of quantum physics tend to be more Leibnizian in this regard, as opposed to the more "ontotheological" string theorists. It has been suggested, for instance, that the best way to describe the collapse of the wave function—in which a quantum resolves itself into a particle and "makes a choice," as it were, between two paths or places—is to say that in such cases the world has split into two incompatible universes, one in which Schrödinger's cat lives and another in which the cat dies. Such universes emerge at every moment in time, or time could be redescribed as the very production of these multiplicities. If we accept this description, however, we must take seriously the trigger involved, the moment when an observation occurs. This observation is very much like Bergson's act of mind, the decision that splits actuality and possibility and constitutes them at the same time.

I hope it will be clear by now that while dealing in a Deleuzian idiom with the problem of time and possible worlds an echo of our reading of Freud has always been present, namely, the reading that focused on the dream work as the unfurling of the path not chosen or even of the impossible path composed of mutually excluded choices present only as the condensations of the signifier. As Deleuze says in *The Fold*, "with its unfurling of divergent series in the same world . . . comes the irruption of incompossibilities on the same stage, where Sextus will rape *and* not rape Lucrecia, where Caesar will cross and not cross the Rubicon, where Fang kills, is killed, and neither kills nor is killed."[54] In this last example he refers to Borges's "Garden of Forking Paths," in which the sinologist Stephen Albert explains to the narrator of the story the nature of the mysterious book written by the narrator's ancestor Ts'ui Pên: "In contrast to Newton and Schopenhauer, your ancestor did not believe in a uniform, absolute time. He believed in an infinite series of times, in a growing and vertiginous network of divergent, convergent, and parallel times. That web of times that draw close, bifurcate, cut across one another, or secularly ignore one another, comprises all possibilities" (Borges 479). As Ts'ui Pên's descendant, the German spy Yu Tsun, listens to Albert he senses all around him the pullulation of these multiple worlds, the house "saturated to the infinite with invisible people." The vision ends with his decision to kill Albert in order to send a secret message to Berlin indicating the name of a city to be bombed, but the story does not end there. Rather, Borges ends his tale with the narrator's confession of remorse: his chief back in Germany "does not know (no one can know) my innumerable contrition and weariness." These last lines, it seems to me, are there to remind us that the decision that renders actuality out of the virtual field of the possible cannot be conceived outside its relation to desire, and the very choice that cuts one path off gives birth to the desire to have followed it.

The accompaniment of divergent series of incompossibilities, the virtual context to our limited actuality, is in many ways exactly how we have articulated the unconscious. Virtuality crystallizes into actuality and potentiality through action or decision. In a very similar way to how Lacan described the retroactive zipping together of meaning following the insertion of an anchoring point into a sentence, the action "pulls and develops the event immediately into denouement, like a cause from which all the different possibilities would crystallize afterwards as its unrealized effects" (Lambert 30).

This action, like the awakening, happens; although we call it a moment of de-*cision*, because it slices, cuts into a flow, it is not at all clear that there is a subject who decides but rather that what we call subject is always composed by a multiplicity of such decisions, or cuts: "A machine may be defined as a system of interruptions or breaks (*coupures*). These breaks should in no way be considered as a separation from reality; rather, they operate along lines that vary according to whatever aspect of them we are considering. Every machine, in the first place, is related to a continual material flow (*hylé*) that it cuts into. . . . Far from being the opposite of continuity, the break or interruption conditions this continuity: it presupposes or defines what it cuts into as an ideal continuity" (*AO* 36). Furthermore, this happening or event of this decision seems to fill a similar function to that which in Lacan's thought we termed the taking of a minimal distance, precisely insofar as both entail the retroactive production of reality, as we have seen in the context of Deleuze's analyses of Bergson and Leibniz. The question that remains is to what extent Deleuze and Guattari's critique of psychoanalysis implies a general rejection of such spacing as being complicit in the sort of massive repression that goes under the name Oedipus.

Gregg Lambert makes the following observation based on a review of the entirety of Deleuze's work: "Throughout his work, Deleuze speculates concerning what would happen if a certain decision were no longer possible, that is, when the symbol of judgment no longer had the power to pull everything into its wake, and time no longer rushes for the door, seeks to actualize itself, to 'actualize itself' or become realized in one duration" (Lambert 30). This is why Deleuze becomes fascinated with the image of hesitation, stammering, "which multiplies possible worlds like the fractal lines of a crystal-event" (Lambert 31). Indeed, what Deleuze objects to is precisely the preemptive and presumptuous judgment that refuses to hesitate and hence itself refuses to space, to allow for the creative backflow of creativity to upset the balance of power, the hegemony of the decisive act. It would seem that secondary interpretation can be deployed in such a way as to shut down the very access to possible worlds that is the motor of creativity; in other words, the very levying of a decisive event that we associate with minimal distance can itself deny such distance, cover it over or fill it up such that primary interpretation is nipped in the bud. As Deleuze says in *Bergsonism*, what appears in the interval is emotion, a "creative emotion that precedes all representation, itself generating new ideas" (*B* 110, qtd. in Lambert 31). To hold that Deleuze's refusal of Oedipalization constitutes an essential refusal of the mediation of otherness would be to ignore the centrality of otherness and specifically of other people throughout

Deleuze's oeuvre. As Deleuze writes with Guattari toward the end of his life, the Other is "the condition of all perception, for others as well as ourselves" (*WP* 18, qtd. in Lambert 35). What Deleuze refuses, and to me it seems rightly so, is the intrusion of a notion of otherness that is limited to the figure of the father's intrusion on an original and ultimately lost satisfaction in the mother's body. Was this not part of psychoanalysis? Most certainly, and nevertheless it is a part that psychoanalysis in my view can do well without. The interpretive string of Freud-Lacan-Deleuze can certainly be read as its own kind of family romance, a Bloomian story of alternatively raging against prior genius or toppling aging fathers, if that is what interests one. The production-oriented philosophy espoused by Deleuze and Guattari is better served, however, when one views this genealogy precisely as an interpretive string, that is, a string in which concepts are transformed, carried over, and as a result new meanings are infused with new potentialities of production and effect. Deleuze famously said of his interpretive style that it consisted of buggering famous philosophers and having them give birth to monsters;[55] can it then be anything other than our obligation to do the same to him?

3

The Purloined String

If Lacan chose his reading of Poe's "The Purloined Letter," published in his *Tales* of 1845, as the leadoff piece to his 1966 *Écrits*, this was because there was something about Poe's story that encapsulated for Lacan the message of his teaching to date. As Lacan writes in the introduction to the 1966 volume, what we decipher in Poe's fiction is "the division where the subject verifies that he is being traversed by an object without either of them penetrating anything."[1] Indeed, this division—which can be that between the subject of the enunciation and that of the statement, between fiction and the truth that inhabits it, or between reality and truth, as we will discuss in greater detail below—can be understood as the centerpiece of Lacan's philosophical contribution, as it was understood to be by Jacques Derrida. Derrida made this seminar the object of an exhaustive critique in a paper originally published in 1975 in the journal *Poétique* under the title "Le facteur de la verité," either "The Factor of Truth" or "Truth's Postman," depending on how you read the play on words. After Lacan's death in 1981, Derrida was invited to speak at a conference on the subject "Lacan and the Philosophers," where he presented a version of what has now been published in English as "For the Love of Lacan." In that piece Derrida largely reiterates the critique of 1975 but also couches it in an homage for what he termed Lacan's unparalleled ability to read "the singular desire of the philosophers." These interventions and the string they comprise are the subject of the following pages.

Death and the Signifier

Two questions that have emerged from the discussion so far concern the relation of spacing to time and the relation of language to reality. As regards the first point, the question may be rightly raised that if one speaks of spacing and of taking a minimal distance, how can this translate into the sort of temporal processes that have occupied much of my argumentation thus far? The best way to understand this phenomenon is to think of the understanding-effect that the figure of a period or full stop can have on the flow of speech or writing. During the time of the listening or reading act, the meaning of a sentence remains suspended; we engage in microhermeneutical guesses, which themselves involve a certain spacing or interruption in the flow but whose main function is to preempt a more radical beat whose purpose is to conclude a thought. Meaning is produced as a temporal and a spatial object in that moment, as having occurred in the past (and being related to the future and the present), as being a nugget of thought, something transmissible, a message, something that exists apart from its transmission between subjects. Indeed part of the emphasis of deconstructive analysis as well as Lacanian thinking on the subject of speech is precisely the demythification of a notion of transmission that would involve the movement of intention to expression to comprehension in a direct fashion. If the model of retroactive fixation of meaning can be said to emerge from a Lacanian paradigm, then it must be insisted that the coherence or fixity of the message so rendered is at least as illusory as the coherence or fixity of the self-image produced in the mirror stage, in which a subject's fundamental sense of self is revealed to depend at the most basic level on a misrecognition produced by its identification with an alienated gaze. In other words, the subject who is thus figured as holder of original and immediate intention is revealed to be the sort of afterimage of the very process of utterance that expresses that ostensible intention. Such a revelation can be viewed negatively, in which case we are treated to the critical aspect of poststructuralist theory whose effect is a kind of implicit nostalgia, as if the original intention thus "lost" were in fact once there and subsequently lost, and it can also be viewed positively as an embracing of the simulacra as such, the sort of yeah-saying to rootlessness or thrownness that connects Nietzsche's and Heidegger's work as well as that of Derrida and Deleuze. In Deleuze's phrase from *Difference and Repetition*, the mask no longer hides a real face; there are only masks all the way down.[2]

The difficulty in this formulation insists in all attempts to philosophize about the loss of the original or the immediate. How can we do this without at the same time instituting that which we are negating? Derrida's beautiful phrase "essential corruptibility" captures what I am speaking about,[3] and its message is consonant with psychoanalysis's repeated insistence that the lost object was never really there in the first place. Nevertheless, psychoanalytic theory can be heard to continue, we mourn its loss. Philosophy may be right in rejecting that mourning as an assertion of a loss that never was, but its very act of refusal can be seen as a way of dealing with such mourning more or less successfully. We mourn the loss of an object we never had, says psychoanalysis, or we are essentially corruptible beings who continue to hold on to the belief that our corruption is secondary, historical. The secondary itself, however, is primary; there can be no primary interpretation without secondary interpretation; minimal distancing is always there; it is the corruption that is our essence. If totalitarianism is the price of loving it too dearly, then psychosis is the price of believing one can refuse it.

This question is not at all irrelevant to the question of the relation of language to reality. In a similar sense, the posing of the question, like the very enunciation of an orientation shared, I believe, by deconstruction, Deleuzian thought, and psychoanalysis, leads us to the unfortunate position of seeming to affirm what we are in fact denying. To deny, for example, that there is a clear distinction to be made between language and reality puts one in the strange position of distinguishing between those very elements one is claiming have no distinction. The result is that one either has to endure a bit of ambiguity, a bit of apparent self-contradiction, or the other option, simply has to speak as if the problem were not there. Ultimately, we often begin by arguing the former and then doing the latter, which I think is exemplary in Deleuze's philosophy.

Let us examine a position that opens up on precisely the problematic we are discussing. Deleuze's philosophy, this position argues, differs radically from psychoanalysis and deconstruction in that these constitute a kind of linguistic fetishism, an insidious denial of the real on the basis of a belief in the ubiquity of the signifier.[4] The problem is, of course, that the assertion not only negates one of the essential tenets of deconstructive and psychoanalytic thought but also seems to put Deleuzian thought precisely in the kind of objectivist tradition it has always criticized: a tradition that thinks of thought as taking place "within" or "alongside" a world[5] or language as referring to an independent reality. The irony is that when Deleuze and Guattari criticize signification, precisely what they are debunking is the referential mode of language, whereby the line of flight inherent in a signifying series is "referred to a supreme signifier representing itself as both lack and excess" (*TP* 117). That the "form of the signifier has a substance . . . namely, the Face" constitutes a reterritorialization of the basic drive of the signifying regime, that "every sign refers to another sign" (*TP* 112). It is crucial to grasp here that the tenor of this critique of "the interpretosis of the priest" is exactly homologous to that of deconstruction's critique of psychoanalysis and specifically to that of Derrida's critique of Lacan: namely, that his system contains a surreptitious and insistent drive to return all desire to a center that is simultaneously the embodiment of presence and of absence. This forced return is exactly what Deleuze and Guattari vilify under the name of interpretation: "The discovery of the psychoanalyst-priest . . . was that interpretation had to be subordinated to signifiance, to the point that the signifier would impart no signified without the signified reimparting signifier in its turn" (*TP* 114). Can we not see in these words precisely the distinction that we have discovered at work in Freud's and Lacan's own texts? Is there not, in the basic drive of signification, according to which a sign refers to another sign, the shuttling back and forth of primary interpretation? Conversely, is not the centering of that movement in an ultimately empty signifier one version of the movement we have called secondary interpretation? Indeed, Deleuze and Guattari would appear to be condemning in what they call the signifying regime the predominance of a particular reterritorializing function, and they are concerned to show that the signifying regime is only one of a multiplicity of regimes of signs.

"Semiotic systems depend on assemblages," they say, and that is why it is absolutely correct to say that signs are machines that interact in the world with other machines, like mouths.[6] What is absolutely wrong is to understand by that utterance that Deleuzian philosophy is somehow about the whole of reality while these other thought systems are stuck within the problematic of signification. This is so *because to read the utterance that way reinstates precisely the division that it erased* and seems to express a world in which the Deleuzian philosopher can hold objects like words and mouths in his or her hand and compare them or fit them together like Legos, as opposed to a world in which the object mouth and the word mouth are understood to be registers of one another, the result of foci or modes of articulation rather than of substantial essence. The object mouth is what is rendered when discussing the imaginary register, the word when discussing the symbolic register. The trick to grasping these registers is to understand that they are precisely that, registers, and not what they are often understood to be: separately existing fields. That said, the resolution of the imaginary as a viable register is the function of what we have been calling secondary interpretation. While it need not be of the totalitarian nature that Deleuze and Guattari impute to it, without it the basic fluidity of primary interpretation is frozen.

Let us specify. The traditional model might stipulate: there is a mouth, and then there is what we say about the mouth, which affects our way of perceiving what was already there. If you deny this you are a silly relativist who would also deny the reality of anything independent of our knowledge of it, and hence you are a throwback to the ridiculous excesses of German idealism. Heidegger has one of the clearest demonstrations of the bankruptcy of this model of thought. The problem with it, he said, was that it reduced being to the accumulation of beings, these already existing objects in the world like mouths, or, to put it in another way, it implicitly put factuality (that there are such and such things) before facticity (that the previous sentence depends on such things being revealed to me in a world in which their existence is already constituted by an immeasurable field of referentiality). The world, as we said, is not encountered out there; it worlds.[7]

The problem with saying "there is a mouth, and then there is what we say about the mouth" is that it involves the deliberate denial of the entire process by which a mouth came to be a mouth, came to be recognized as having certain functions, came to be part of the fabric of the world. It is the process of this coming to be part of the fabric of the world that Heidegger calls language. Again, to belittle this insight by calling it a humanism, for example, assumes the very distinction that this thought does not allow and that the critics of humanism would be well advised to disallow as well, namely, the distinction between a human perspective on the world and that non-human world that exists out there and encompasses us. Deleuze's philosophy makes no sense if one reads it as reiterating this distinction. The fact that it sometimes sounds that way is due to Deleuze's speaking from within an understanding that has already definitively refused it.

I argue the same concerning the thought of Lacan: it makes no sense if it is read as reiterating this distinction, although it must be admitted that at times it is the hardest of three discourses to read consistently in this other fashion. What does he mean, for example, when he differentiates the language of bees from the dimension of language as such, as he does in the seminar on "The Purloined Letter"? The utterance would seem again to presuppose exactly the distinction we should be wary of, that there is a bee way of seeing the world and a human way that we can somehow objectively distinguish. The point, I think, lies somewhere else. The language of bees, in which a highly variegated series of movement indicates for other bees the exact location of a field of flowers, for instance, is in Lacan's words "only an imaginary function more differentiated than others."[8] The distinction seems to rest in the notion of naturally given objects, which for Lacan means that so-called animal communication—or a form of communication entirely expressible in imaginary terms—turns on objects held in common or a geography inhabited simultaneously by various members. Armed with an imaginary function "more differentiated than others," a bee can communicate distance and direction into movement and thereby transmit that information to other bees, insofar as they inhabit the same geography. "But such communication is not transmissible in symbolic form. It may be maintained only in the relation with the object" (*PL* 35). If the realm of exactitude is distinguished from that of truth, it is precisely insofar as the statement of a bee could never involve a judgment of truth but only of accuracy, whereas the question of truth is situated "at the foundation of intersubjectivity." Lacan illustrates this foundation as being precisely that moment at which the reception of an utterance becomes dependent on a question of intent. A speaker's message to me is accompanied by an implicit question back to the speaker concerning the intention of that message, such that—in a scenario radically different from any form of purely imaginary communication—we can lie to one another by merely telling the truth.[9] The fact that Lacan theorizes this implicit questioning about intention, which itself is an instantiation of what Deleuze and Guattari criticized as the despotism of the Face, as operative in symbolic communication, does not, however, mean that the Face or the intention in fact determines the message, as we will discuss further on.

The theory of intersubjectivity suggests that subjective position takes place via a "decision . . . reached in a glance's time" (*PL* 32).[10] No longer are we dealing with a content expressible in terms of shared objective space; now what is at stake depends on what the other may or may not see. The question of the other's viewpoint vis-à-vis ourselves is central, formative to our actions. The play of glances and how they structure an intersubjective field is a function of what Lacan calls, in his reading of Poe's story, the letter, but what I want to stress here is that the letter has very clearly in Lacan's scenario no representative function; rather, it functions as a point of orientation. The letter is deliberately chosen in this interpretation as a physical thing that moves around. What is specific about this object, moreover, is that it is "endowed with the property of *nullibeity*" (*PL* 38), that is, of being nowhere existent. It is there and yet not there at the same time, or rather it is there and its existence has nothing to do with its presence because what is at stake is its function as orientation for an intersubjective space. When we consider things in the register of the imaginary alone, there is no object that functions in that way; this functioning is proper to the symbolic order and hence language per se. But once such a function has become permissible, once we have revealed the existence of the symbolic, then what we realize is that our capture in the symbolic is manifested along imaginary lines (*PL* 28); that is, there is no separability between the two registers, only between two modes of description.

The signifier is singular in many ways (*PL* 38–39). It does not admit of partition to begin with, which is to say that it acts as a *trait unaire* or unifying trait. Imaginary reality is always bound by signifiers in that multiple experience latches onto singular expression. In other words, rather than repeating the cliché that a picture is worth a thousand words, we should insist on its opposite, that a word is worth or can represent a thousand pictures. Imaginary experience is what it is, but "we cannot say of the purloined letter, unlike other objects, that it must be *or* not be in a particular place but that unlike them it will be and not be where it is, wherever it goes."

The police who search for the letter in the queen's apartment are likened to philosophers, to metaphysicians who "have such an immutable notion of the real that they fail to notice that their search transforms it into its objects" (*PL* 39), exactly as Heidegger's physical ontologists failed to notice that their search for being transformed it into objects. As they hone in on the smallest cracks and crevices, as they divide space into smaller and smaller compartments in their search, "do we not," asks Lacan, "see space itself shed its leaves like a letter" (*PL* 39)? Poe's policemen, like the philosophers, search an imaginary realm already structured by the symbolic as if it were an imaginary realm, a shared geography, unaltered by the symbolic.[11] They search like the atomists for that element that refuses to sunder, that will call an end to the search, that will not refer us further. What they fail to see is that they are looking for a letter and hence looking in the wrong place.

The letter is not found because unlike things in the imaginary, for which place never becomes a question, in the symbolic it is always a question, and hence things can become lost; everything can become lost or purloined. (We lose things when we feel they should be somewhere where they are not, a symbolic determination.) That is, their path of movement between others and ourselves is prolonged, and that prolongation we sometimes call life. Life, in other words, is being lost or misplaced, which is why metaphysical interpretations of philosophy are all about finding it, ourselves, the truth, the letter. As Heidegger argues in division II of *Being and Time*, however, the task of finding oneself and hence of completing oneself is identical to a drive toward death because it is only in death that the dynamic becoming that is Dasein achieves the kind of stasis in which it can encompass itself as an object, but at which point it ultimately misrecognizes itself because in becoming a dead thing it is no longer Dasein (*BT* 221–24). That is to say, such a drive is indeed a death drive, and this drive underlies the work of mourning we discussed above, but at the same time neither death nor any dream of plenitude can offer that final fulfillment. The prolongations of the signifier are what we call life, but only insofar as the signifier "materializes the agency of death" (*PL* 38) as a drive, as the fundamental drive, and as the possibility of our utter inexistence that presents itself as the doorway to fulfillment.

"The Purloined Letter," in Lacan's hands, would seem then to be a parable of philosophy, a story about how we think about truth and reality and the sorts of dead end streets that philosophers can take and where those dead ends do or do not lead them. But if the letter or truth can be diverted, as Lacan says, it must—so the logic goes, and it is a logic we have been resisting—"*have a course that is proper to it*: the trait by which its incidence as signifier is affirmed" (*PL* 43). Yet like thinking authentically, for Heidegger, or like doing philosophy well (as we will discuss in the next chapter), the propriety of this course is precisely not the return to or revival of something lost but rather "the trait by which its incidence as signifier is affirmed," its incidence, that is, as that element that always refuses an ultimate resting place. Like the ultimate word that the narrator of Borges's story "UNDR" searches for, its meaning is nothing other than another word: "I grabbed the harp and sang with a different word. 'It is well,' the other said. And I had to approach him to hear. 'You have understood.' "[12] Its propriety, in other words, is to be improper. For this is the essence of repetition: that we arrange our imaginary reality in such a way as to redeem from a barren signifier the return its elemental stature seems to promise, just as the objectivist philosopher seeks in the imaginary world of nature the truth as correspondence to that signifier whose ultimate repetition is nothing other than a meaningless thud and an empty, a priori, and utterly tautological truth.

What, then, of the one who is steadfast in one's pursuit of that truth as object, who tries to grasp the signifier to possess it, to own it and hence place oneself in the position "that no one is in fact capable of assuming, since it is imaginary, that of absolute master" (*PL* 47)? He or she will find that

it cannot become actual without vanishing in the process—but in that case the letter exists as a means of power only through the final assignations of the pure signifier, namely: by prolonging its diversion, making it reach whomever it may concern through a supplementary transfer, that is, by an additional act of treason whose effects the letter's gravity makes it difficult to predict—or indeed by destroying the letter, the only sure means . . . of being rid of what is destined by nature to signify the annulment of what it signifies. (*PL* 46)

The letter, in other words, is identical to its eternal referral, which Lacan here calls the final assignations of the pure signifier; it can only reach whomever it may concern, that is, its anonymous addressee, through a supplementary transfer, by going through always one more digression, an act of treason to the original intent or final destinatory. Indeed, it reaches its destination by an act of destruction because its destiny is precisely to signify the annulment of what it signifies, that is, of itself, of its very an-nulment. Because its only function is to signify something other, anything other, philosophy's quest to find in it truth as identity or self-presence is doomed by a fatal and wonderful irony, namely, that it is seeking there the only thing it cannot find.

What remains, Lacan asks, of a signifier "when it has no more signi-fication" (*PL* 51)? We ask this question of the signifier and its answer defers us yet again, giving us only the pieces of a splintered imaginary, "the frag-mentation of your shattered childhood. . . . [S]uch will be your feast until the return of the stone guest I shall be for you since you call me forth" (*PL* 52). We challenge the signifier to give up its truth, and what we get is the feast of our own selves and the silence of the grave. Does a letter always ar-rive at its destination? The answer is as clear and ultimately as incompre-hensible as the certainty of our own death.

Truth to the Letter

The engagement at hand is about the concept of truth. It is my con-tention that a very different notion of truth is capable of emerging from the "Seminar on the Purloined Letter" than the one Derrida seeks there, the one he finds there, just as Lacan in his reading finds the truth, or better, his discourse positions him as "in general proffering the discourse on truth, the truth on truth."[13] For Derrida's reading, the concept of truth is reinstated in the seminar in its full metaphysical glory, first in the classical form of *adaequatio intellectus et rei*, and second in the incorporation of the Heideg-gerian discourse of veiling/unveiling (*PT* 193). The notion of truth, which is indeed at stake in this seminar, far from being reinstated into said tradi-tion, is rather subjected to a re-interpretation that pulls both *adaequatio* and veiling/unveiling into its wake, that tries to explain, in other words, why these forms of truth arise.

That said, it must be recognized that Derrida's reading is character-istically long and that it is a reading of far more than Lacan's seminar. A good portion of that reading is in fact a reading of Poe's story, with an ex-plicit claim that it is Lacan's failure to read the story well that leads in some way to a more general failure, a failure to articulate a vision of truth that escapes the metaphysical tradition: "Literary writing, here, is brought into an illustrative position: 'to illustrate' here meaning to read the general law in the example, to make clear the meaning of a law or of a truth" (*PT* 178). By failing to focus on the writing of the story, on its narration and its various frame, in other words, the seminar's "interest in the agency of the signifier in its letter seizes upon this agency to the extent that it constitutes, precisely, on the first approach, the exemplary content, the meaning, the written of Poe's fiction, as opposed to its writing, its signifier, and its narrating form" (*PT* 179). It is the rebuttal of Barbara Johnson that this is a somewhat paradoxical critique because it must do exactly the same to Lacan's text as it argues Lacan's does to Poe's in order to make this claim. Still, I am less interested in the justice of the matter than in the matter, or the so-called materiality of the signifier, that lies at the heart of the debate, insofar as the notion of truth "provides the Seminar with its rigorously philosophical import" (*PT* 178). Lacan's reading of Poe, in other words, is certainly inadequate as a reading of Poe; Derrida's reading, for other reasons, while brilliant as a reading of Poe, is inadequate as a reading of Lacan.

The general form of the philosophical misreading to which Derrida submits Lacan's seminar is as follows: statements concerning truth that are best, most consistently, most productively read as *redefining the notion of truth as regards other discursive elements*, Derrida reads instead as *defining or situating those discursive elements in relation to an immobile and received notion of truth*: " 'Truth inhabits fiction' cannot be understood in the somewhat perverse sense of a fiction more powerful than the truth which inhabits it, the truth that fiction inscribes within itself. In truth, the truth inhabits fiction as the master of the house, as the law of the house, as the economy of fiction. The truth executes the economy of fiction, directs, organizes, and makes possible fiction: 'It is that truth, let us note, which makes the very existence of fiction possible' " (*PT* 178). Quoting exactly the same passage twice in the space of a page could be read either as obsessive quoting or as signaling the weight, the emphasis, the passage is due. It is due such emphasis in Derrida's reading because of its apparently straightforward claim: "truth makes fiction possible," a clear establishment of hierarchy and dependence, with something called truth at the top of the totem.

This excessive quotation also nevertheless reveals a strategy, for I refuse to believe anyone of Derrida's intelligence would have misread this point inadvertently: Derrida here exchanges, in the idiom of classical language philosophy, use for mention. Where Derrida reads that truth makes fiction possible, Lacan's texts speaks of "that truth," namely, the truth that "it is the symbolic order which is constitutive for the subject" (*PL* 29). In other words, because the symbolic order is constitutive for the subject and because truth is this constitution, fiction is possible. This truth, because it is attached in its fate to the symbolic order, is not about *adaequatio* but about positioning. Fiction depends on what Irving Goffman and Luiz Costa Lima have called the keying of a frame relative to an exterior frame;[14] this process is symbolic insofar as the frame keyed is marked by a signifier as being suspended beyond judgments of truth and falsity, and the same signifier that marks that border thereby marks an implicit realm of truth. Insofar as there is fiction there is truth, or the suspended judgment of truth is what makes our very notion of fiction possible.

The seminar is indeed, then, about truth, but it is not about the truth Derrida claims it is about, and Derrida's refusal to understand that truth is here defined as a matter of positioning leads him to misread everything about the seminar's argument, right down to the supposed circularity of the signifier, which grounds his reading of truth as *adaequatio* in Lacan's theory.

Lacan leads us back to the truth, to a truth which itself cannot be lost. He brings us back to the letter, shows us that the letter brings itself back toward its *proper* place via a *proper* itinerary, and, as he overtly notes, it is this destination which interests him, destiny as destination. The signifier has its place in the letter, and the letter refinds its proper meaning in its proper place. A certain reappropriation and a certain readequation will reconstitute the proper, the place, meaning, and truth that have become distant from themselves for the time of a detour or a non-delivery. . . . But what the Seminar insists upon showing, finally, is that there is a single proper itinerary of the letter which returns to a determinable place that is always the same and that is its own; and that . . . the meaning of the letter and the sense of its itinerary are necessary, unique, and determinable in truth, that is, as truth. (*PT* 182)

Truth, therefore, inhabits fiction and is its master and does so insofar as it determines the itinerary of the letter and hence its meaning as necessary, as unique. Is it not possible, however (and indeed, I will now argue, a more convincing reading), that Lacan's thesis concerning truth is *not* that it is the immutable place that determines the itinerary of the signifier? Is it not much more in conformity with the entire drive of his writing to argue that truth is a symbolic function that arises inevitably, perhaps, but nevertheless as a result of the itinerary of a letter that is itself never necessary, never determined by some pre-existing truth but rather itself the vector that defines truth as such? The whole of Derrida's argument lies in the assumption that "the search for a restitution of the object" (*PT* 183) is in fact a search for and restitution of an object that psychoanalysis believes in, believes that it actually exists out there in the world somewhere or in the past. This is a useful argument if your point is to argue the opposite because it would seem to imply that you, the arguer, thought the non-existence of this object first. Of course, to argue this you would need to repress the history of a psychoanalytic thinking that, for reasons of its own, at first in total innocence of the urgency of such questions for philosophy, denied that such an original fulfilling object had ever existed. It is not that it was there and then was lost and now the signifier magically returns to that place of loss, "the unveiled site of the lack of a penis, as the truth of the phallus, that is of castration" (*PT* 183), as Derrida reads. On the contrary, there is the letter and the letter follows a procession, a *défilé*, as Lacan calls it, whose truly unpredictable stopping points are retroactively conceived as destinations of the letter and hence destiny. As Lacan puts it elsewhere:

This is not to say that there is nothing to be gained from the different meanings uncovered in the general march of history along the path which runs from Bossuet (Jacques-Bénigne) to Toynbee (Arnold), and which is punctuated by the edifices of Auguste Comte and Karl Marx. Everyone knows very well that they are worth as little for directing research into the recent past as they are for making any reasonable presumptions about the events of tomorrow. Besides, they are modest enough to postpone their certainties until the day after tomorrow, and not too prudish either to admit the retouching that permits predictions about what happened yesterday.[15]

From one perspective, it is nothing short of astonishing that Derrida could advance the reading he does, because that reading would seem so obvious. We hardly need a philosopher of Derrida's sophistication to tell us that what one of the world's most notoriously difficult and obscure writers means by "a letter always arrives at its destination" is precisely what he would appear to be saying and what a child could understand: that the destination precedes and awaits the letter as its destiny.

Yet what does Lacan actually write? The use of the letter

for the ends of power can only be potential, since it cannot become actual without vanishing in the process—but in that case the letter exists as a means of power only through the final assignations of the pure signifier, namely: by prolonging its diversion, making it reach whomever it may concern through a supplementary transfer, that is, by an additional act of treason whose effects the letter's gravity makes it difficult to predict—or indeed by destroying the letter, the only sure means . . . of being rid of what is destined by nature to signify the annulment of what it signifies. (*PL* 46)

The letter, then, as I stressed in the last chapter, is identical to its eternal referral, which Lacan here calls the final assignations of the pure signifier; it can only reach whomever it may concern, that is, its anonymous and utterly contingent addressee, through a supplementary transfer, by going through always one more digression, an act of treason to any notion of original intent or of final destinatory. Indeed, it reaches its destination only by an act of destruction because its destiny is precisely to signify the annulment of what it signifies, that is, of itself, of its very annulment. To reiterate—in contrast to Derrida's reading—my conclusion from the previous chapter: the Seminar is a parable of philosophy and of the philosopher's search for truth. If the letter's only function is to signify something other, anything other, then philosophy's quest to find in it truth as identity or self-presence is doomed in that it is seeking there the only thing it cannot find.

 Yet what of the argument, cited above, that the very notion of diversion explicit in Lacan's etymological appropriation of purloined, prolonged, *en souffrance*, requires by default that there be a proper path and hence a place to which the letter returns? If the letter or truth can be diverted, as Lacan says, it must "*have a course that is proper to it*: the trait by which its incidence as signifier is affirmed" (*PL* 43). But what authorizes us to read this propriety as a return? What if the proper course of the signifier is precisely not to return, to do anything but return? In fact, the proper course, Lacan says, is precisely not the return to or revival of something lost but specifically "the trait by which its incidence as signifier is affirmed," its incidence, that is, as that element that always refuses an ultimate resting place. To reiterate, the essence of repetition is to arrange imaginary reality so as to redeem from the signifier the return it has promised, just as the philosopher seeks in the imaginary world that correspondence to the signifier whose final repetition is a meaningless thud, an empty, a priori, and tautological truth. That is the response of truth as *adaequatio*, and the *reductio* of *adaequatio* finds, I feel, no better expression than in the image of a room full of philosopher police who in their search for a letter set to divvying up space until it sheds its leaves like the pages of a book.

Let us try to be clearer. What are the police in Poe's story looking for? We say a letter, but they seem unaware of what a letter might look like. They are searching for something symbolic in an imaginary place, if you will, like realists looking for Dennett's lost sock center or the curious soul seeking to know, to really know, the exact number of times she has blinked in her life. What drives them is, to put it in psychoanalytic terms, a repetition compulsion. They say they seek reality but what they want is to repeat, because that is what the letter promises. The letter separates place from place, time from time. It is only through the letter that things can be lost and hence that they can have a place, Lacan says, and the reason for this is not that the letter has a place but that place, propriety, and the possibility of return are effects of the letter, of the fact that when all else can be divided or partitioned, the letter cannot.

"And this is why," Derrida pounces, "the motivated, never demonstrated presupposition of the materiality of the letter as indivisibility is indispensable for this restricted economy, this circulation of the proper" (*PT* 185). Again, the jubilation seems too facile. Can the thinker who in 1956 gave the address that would become "The Agency of the Letter," in which Saussure's tree is made to splinter into a thousand directions, upward and outward on the intertwined axes of the paradigmatic and the syntagmatic,[16] really mean what Derrida seems to take him to mean when he says that letters do not admit of partition? The letter is deliberately chosen, in this story, as a physical thing that moves around. What is specific about this object, as I have said, is that it is "endowed with the property of nullibeity," of being nowhere existent (*PL* 38). Lacan attributes the word nullibeity to John Wilkins and points out in a footnote that this is the same Wilkins that Jorge Luis Borges writes about "in works which harmonize so well with the phylum of our subject" (*PL* 53). In the piece in question, "The Analytic Language of John Wilkins," Borges describes Wilkins's search for a language free of indeterminacy in that each part of each word has a direct relation to an object in the world: "The word *salmon* doesn't say anything to us; *zana*, the corresponding expression, defines (for the man versed in the forty categories and in the genres of these categories) a scaly river fish of a reddish color" (Borges, III 86). The point to grasp here is that both Lacan and Borges are parodying the idea of a language without indeterminacy, a language in which each element would have its corresponding piece of reality. Unlike the elements of such an impossible language, the signifier is singular because it does not admit of partition, which is to say that it acts as a *trait unaire*, a single trait latching onto multiple experiences: "we cannot say of the purloined letter, unlike other objects, that it must be *or* not be in a particular place but that unlike them it will be and not be where it is, wherever it goes" (*PL* 39).

Derrida sees in this insistence on materiality and indivisibility a residue of metaphysics, of ideality: "*This 'materiality,' deduced from an indivisibility found nowhere, in fact corresponds to an idealization.* Only the ideality of a letter resists destructive division" (*PT* 194). Further on: "He considers the letter only at the point at which it is determined (no matter what he says) by its content of meaning, by the ideality of the message that it 'vehiculates,' by the speech whose meaning remains out of the reach of partition, so that it can circulate, intact, from its place of detachment to its place of reattachment, that is, to the same place. In fact, this letter does not only escape partition, it escapes movement, it does not change its place" (*PT* 194). It would seem that the most poignant moment in this quoted passage is the parenthetical "(no matter what he says)," for it indeed requires an enormous power of concentration to ignore what is in fact said in the seminar enough to come to such remarkable conclusions. Derrida claims that the letter is considered only as meaning, and hence ideality, and that this is what remains out of the reach of partition. This is frankly absurd. As I have made clear already it is precisely meaning that shatters and splinters into every possible direction that is infinitely divisible. What remains is a shell, a form, a mark. Meanings do not circulate, letters do, and in their circulations they provoke myriad new meanings, never traceable back to an original one. Finally, far from returning to the same place, the letter's movement is what marks a place as place in the first place, and if it returns, it will never be to the same place.[17]

Does it not then belong "to the structure of the letter to be capable, always, of not arriving[?] And without this threat . . . [is it not the case that] the circuit of the letter would not even have begun?" (*PT* 187). Indeed, were it not for this very threat, that the letter will not arrive at its destination, there would, quite obviously, be no issue about truth, for *what is truth but that very concept whose emergence is a response to, not merely the threat that a letter does not arrive, but to its very failure to arrive.* Here we can go so far as to say that Derrida is not being quite radical enough: to the extent that it is or could be an issue of a sender's intention, we would have to insist that no letter ever makes or has made it. But then again, no sender really takes this seriously. The reason we do not is that a destinatory is produced, however haphazard, however unsatisfactory; we feel we have been heard; a message has come back to us. What do we hear? Something to the tune of, "Come again?" So we do.

The Racketeer of Truth

Let us leave aside for the moment the question of the ethical import of holding onto certain concepts in order to change them or appropriate them for a new purpose versus replacing them entirely with new concepts. Obviously both operations have something to do with interpretation, perhaps the former only slightly more obviously than the latter. We will come back to this question, as central to our guiding question as it is to the troubled relation between Lacan and Derrida. The way to this question, it seems to me, must pass through another question, other but related, which is that of the position of the one who speaks or writes. Both Derrida and Lacan take up this issue in a way that makes it loom large in their dispute with one another, although they take it up in exceedingly obscure ways. Fifteen years after the publication of his critique of Lacan's seminar and nine years after Lacan's death, Derrida appeared at a colloquium dedicated to the issue of "Lacan and the philosophers," an appearance he agreed to make as an homage to Lacan, as he says. During his speech he reiterates that critique (which he denies is a critique), which despite the mellowed tone and protestations of love for Lacan continues to evidence the same degree of philosophical suspicion as it did in the earlier text. Among the generous utterances he allows as to the importance of Lacan's thought, however, there is one that strikes me as a promising entrée into this question of positioning: "Instead, he staged the singular desire of the philosopher and thereby contributed considerably to opening the space for a sort of new philosophical culture. In which we are situated, despite efforts to make us forget it so as to turn back the clock."[18]

To stage the singular desire of the philosopher was, I must agree with Derrida, at the heart of Lacan's project, and it is also a compelling way to describe the work being done in that seminar I described as being a parable of philosophy because that parable consisted of an analysis of the philosopher's desire, or the desire of a philosophy bent on mistaking truth's symbolic value for an imaginary thing in the world. Such a desire, Lacan goes on to say, is also a desire to speak from a position of absolute mastery because it would be a position that held the letter as something ultimately identified, self-identical, which it cannot be because its very resistance of partition makes it always only identifiable as something other than what it is.

Yet how often philosophers speak from precisely such a position! In fact, one might go so far as to point out the extraordinary difficulty involved in not speaking from that position when one tries, as philosophy must try to do, to generalize about something called truth. Let us attempt a cabaret version of the history of philosophy in one sentence: philosophy is born when the first philosopher asks not whether something is true in a given time and place but what Truth itself is regardless of time and place, and after many generations of frustrating inquiry his descendents come to the conclusion that this was a very good example of question begging, and suggest that truth is in fact merely a description of time and place, at which point they are stymied by the question of whether that conclusion, which seemed to offer such a promising end to ages of painful hand wringing, was the Truth they had always been looking for or merely truth in this secondary, mildly disappointing sense. Now, whereas twentieth-century philosophy has come up with many creative ways of disavowing this problem (i.e., the late-Wittgenstinian way, in which one is essentially scolded for having mistaken an adjective for a noun in the first place), what Derrida here praises Lacan for is having paid attention to the philosopher's desire: what is it about that desire that inspires the philosopher to ask such questions? Rather than attempt to solve the conundrum, then, what Lacan offers is a schematic breakdown of structures of enunciation whose purpose is to articulate the desire involved in the posing of the conundrum. In this schema, what is revealed is that the search to define truth or to say something true about truth is a highly specified instantiation of the desire to embody a place that cannot be embodied, namely, to occupy with the subject of one's utterance, "I," the place of the enunciation of that utterance or, more broadly, to iron away the difference from self at the heart of any and all identity.

The impossibility of occupying this place becomes for Lacan the philosophical template of desire, and it is here that one of Derrida's most strident critiques can be heard because, as he points out, such a move reinstalls at the center of philosophical desire exactly the same structure that was always there, "the circular return of reappropriation toward what is most proper about the proper place, whose borders are circumscribed by lack, and so forth, through a handling of philosophical reference whose form, at least, was in the best of cases elliptical and aphoristic, and the worst, dogmatic" (*RP* 54). In other words, Lacan's model seems to reinstall at the center of all searches a hole, a castration, whose filling in is what we all seek. Let us follow the Lacanian model a bit further, however, to see if this critique holds water. We must begin by recognizing, and there should be no problem to this, that in no place in this psychoanalytic schema of philosophical desire is there the slightest indication that a unified utterance structure is even remotely possible; in fact, it is far more easily recognized that according to this schema such a unity is constitutively impossible because it would require of the signifier that one thing that the signifier cannot be without ceasing to be signifier, namely, to be self-identical or to submit to partition.[19] The coming into being of a being who is in this way submitted to the dictates of signification, Lacan theorizes, involves a certain assumption of powerlessness: I wish to do such and such, I cannot, and so on. The proliferation of these utterances of powerlessness implicates, again logically, the existence of an "I" who can, who easily finds its vehicle in another party. Psychoanalysis, according to normative family practices, assigned this role to the father in recognition of his ability, perhaps in practice, to deny access to the mother for the child while allowing it for himself. The scenario is highly culturally specific, but the Lacanian version generalizes it into a function and reinterprets the vocabulary of psychoanalysis into this description of function: the father is an instantiation of a function, that of being the one who seems to be able to do whatever "I" cannot, and because this constitutive inability is itself a reinterpretation of castration, the paternal function's redefinition involves being a vehicle, as Lacan calls it, for the phallus.

From the perspective of the "castrated I," the father would thus appear to be the one who speaks from the position of plenitude, of total identity between his utterance and the body that utters it, so that his word is self-identical in the way that the word of the "I" can never be. The father himself, on the other hand, or anyone who attains that position vis-à-vis another, cannot fail to know that he is just as powerless as the one who so regards him and that this point of power, this "place of the absolute master," if it exists at all, must be occupied by someone else.[20] Thus does the movement of occupying that place always defer the ultimate status of resident to someone else, an eternal deferral to the authority of some big Other, what we have called that absolutely certain place of absolute uncertainty. It is in the context of this schema that we can now make sense of Lacan's strange comment to Derrida on the occasion of their "second and last encounter," when he allegedly called Derrida "a father who does not recognize . . . the way he himself disregarded the Other [big O] by playing dead." The comment puzzles Derrida, who goes on to say, "I have always wondered whether he didn't mean to say the son, if he didn't want to play the son, to make me or himself into the son, to make of me the son who disregards the Other by playing dead, as he put it, or make himself into the son" (*RP* 51). Yet when we recall, from precisely that seminar on the "Purloined Letter" that so troubles Derrida, that the only position from which the letter does not defer to another is the position of its annihilation or death, then it becomes clear what Lacan was saying: something about the structure of Derrida's utterance, his philosophy, struck Lacan as implicating him in a position of a father who himself fails to recognize that what and how he speaks depends on a disregard for the Other, one that is only possible if one is in fact dead and hence a self-identical thing.[21]

If this is an accurate reading, however, what a strange critique to level against the ultimate destroyer of all and any such position-taking, the one whose discourse never ceases "to deconstruct the privilege of presence, at least as consciousness and egological consciousness" (*RP* 55)! Nevertheless, it is precisely this charge that we must explore if we are to grasp the philosophical difference between these two parties. Let us take as an example Derrida's criticism of the problematic notion of "full speech": "Thus 'full speech' . . . 'is defined through its identity with that of which it speaks.' This point is very important for me . . . because it links phonologocentrism or phallolocentrism to the analytic situation without technical interposition, without an archiving apparatus of repetition, without essential iterability: a very old philosopheme, from Plato up to and including

Heidegger" (*RP* 58). Let us refer to the definition that Derrida quotes earlier from Lacan: "I might as well be categorical: in psychoanalytic matters it is not a question of reality, but of truth, because the effect of full speech is to reorder past contingencies by conferring on them the sense of necessities to come . . . such as they are constituted by the little freedom through which the subject makes them present" (*RP* 58). Reading this statement carefully, it seems to me, puts the lie to a reading of "full speech" as an instance of phonocentrism, if only because it is clear that the necessity invoked by the dimension of truth is constituted through an illusion. This is produced by conferring a sense of necessity on what are (for us) contingencies, a necessity itself dependent on the "freedom" through which the subject makes them present—namely, the de-liberation of self-reflexive narration—a taking distance from the self's immersion in reality that constitutes that imaginary reality at an always minimal distance from the deliberating self. It is of course this very scenario that is enacted during analysis, in the space of the transference, which is at heart the enactment of an illusion that we think is real, that we mistake for a reality.

This reading, however, goes beyond being merely a nitpicking correction of Derrida's interpretation and in fact constitutes the heart of the Lacanian theory of positionality. *The analytic position, or the position of the analyst, insofar as it constitutes an attempt in dialogue to establish a truth, be it of an individual or a philosophical kind, invariably requires the referral to an illusory position of plenitude.* Failure to include this absolute explicitly in the schema translates into an implicit assumption of that position on the part of the speaker. This is, I believe, the lesson that Lacan drew from Hegel: to historicize being, to narrativize the contingencies of one's own life or of the history of philosophy in the search of a truth about one's own life or about philosophy, one must speak as if there existed a position of absolute knowledge, of totality. This position for some "us" infinitely deferred coincides with exactly what is, in itself.[22] At the same time, this very utterance of certainty is accompanied by the equal and opposing certainty that the existence of such a place coincides exactly with the impossibility of our ever occupying it. To utter a discourse of pure temporality, to speak in such a way as to utter the truth about temporality, namely, that "a letter *can* always *not* arrive at its destination" (*RP* 65), is to disregard the Other, to play dead, to implicitly believe that this letter has arrived so that all others may not, but without saying it. To say the opposite, to say that a letter "always arrives at its destination" while at the same time recalling that one cannot ever occupy the destination that could verify that truth, recalling, in other words, the dependence of truth on the fictive production of necessity out of contingency, is ultimately to deny to oneself the position of *facteur de la verité*. One denies it by assuming it, all the while, in a duplicitous fashion, denying that it can be assumed at all, because to deny it outright is to assume it in practice.

This conclusion has serious implications for a discussion of interpretation, and with this I come back to the issue with which I opened this chapter: whether it is preferable to re-interpret old concepts or to invent new ones. Those of us who make use of psychoanalysis are certainly under a lot of philosophical pressure to replace outmoded concepts, perhaps even more so than in other fields of inquiry, and the reason should be clear. We come consistently, and often justifiably, under the criticism that our concepts have lost their ability to enlighten and now function merely as part of the very repressive apparatus they once sought to—or at least purported to—undermine. How can one criticize phallocentrism when one still makes use of the term *phallus*? How can one engage in progressive sexual politics when one obsessively locates castration at the heart of desire? How can one leave metaphysics behind or even conceive of one's work as participating in a general critique of metaphysical thinking if one conceives of desire as the search for an original lost plenitude? In my own work I insist on taking religious discourse seriously, and not just banishing it with other outmoded talk into one of the several dustbins of history.[23] Why is this so?

It seems to me that the ultimate reason for such terminological recycling has everything to do with the previous discussion. By initiating a discourse with the radical rejection of the concepts that form the ground or field of my discourse, I may be responding to a correct intuition regarding the status of these concepts while at the same time failing to recognize the way they function within the enunciative structure of that discourse. The terms in question—for example, being, truth, the father, castration—insofar as they are transmitted as constants, the fundamental elements guarding the coherence of a given discourse, have themselves precisely the value within those discourses of absolutely certain points of absolute uncertainty or, to put it in another vocabulary, quilting points. They are fictional and at the same time operative insofar as their fictional deployment is what makes these vocabularies function as tools of inquiry into something called truth, the specific truth that discourse aims at. While it is a fundamental mistake to reify these concepts, that is, to treat them as something whose nature can be sought out in the imaginary, it is equally a mistake to underestimate their importance, to foreclose them or simply replace them without making the necessary effort to rearticulate an understanding of the work they do within a system. To foreclose them or replace them does not merely run the risk of destroying a system of thought which might after all be desirable; the risk is far more drastic, namely, that of installing the speaker in the place of certainty in the very same breath with which one denounces the uncertainty of all other positions. To be perfectly clear, this is not a mere denunciation of the relativism of self-defeating negation. I am perfectly aware that the negation of absolute truth is not self-refuting (because the notion of truth thereby deployed is no longer that of the objectivist who would make such a critique).[24] The reason it is not self-refuting is that the speaker's position is inevitably, irrevocably duplicitous. He must deny what he asserts even while asserting it, and to fail to assert the truth under denial is to assert oneself, the very position from which one speaks, as being nonduplicitous, unitary, and utterly truthful.

I believe the realization of this conundrum is part of the reason why there has been a kind of rapprochement in recent years between deconstruction and psychoanalysis, on the one hand, and between deconstruction, once so determinedly atheistic, and certain strains of philosophical theology. To recall a refrain from the first chapter, in Kierkegaard's words, the paradox of mediation cannot be mediated, and this, I theorized, was as good a formulation as any of what Lacanian theory calls the real, the unsymbolizable, the distance, perhaps, between some inassimilable truth and the one who looks toward it, desires it, and by desiring it keeps it open and unrealized. One can, of course, philosophize that truth away with a rigor so profound it confounds comprehension. That is not the risk or the downfall. It is, rather, that in denouncing the purveyor of truth we become, ourselves, exactly that.

4

The Temporality String

The discussion thus far has led to the stipulation that there is no way to consider in full the problem of interpretation without broaching the philosophical question of time. There is no doubt that the subject of time is among the most belabored in the history of philosophy and has been called by more than one thinker the essential philosophical problem.[1] As Borges once recounted: "an Argentine philosopher and I were conversing about time, and the philosopher said, 'We have made a lot of progress in that over the last few years.' And I thought that if I had asked him about space, he certainly would have answered, 'We have made a lot of progress in that over the last few blocks.'"[2] Given this centrality and apparent intractability of the question of time, the approach in this chapter cannot help but suffer from selective attention. That said, the texts that form this temporality string are, in my mind, among the most profound considerations of the problem in the twentieth century. Aided by a supporting cast, the principal figures in this string are Jorge Luis Borges, Martin Heidegger, and Jacques Derrida, although the notion of "time as spacing" (in Derrida's formulation) that I will be deriving from their texts will be shown to have its most productive correlate in the Lacanian model we have developed thus far. Borges publishes "Funes the Memorious" in his *Ficciones* of 1944, in the middle of a career whose most prominent philosophical obsession will be that of time. Martin Heidegger will move time to the center of twentieth-century philosophical concerns in his opus *Being and*

Time in 1927 and two years later in his *Kant and the Problem of Metaphysics*. The former, however, and specifically a footnote from that text will form the basis for one of the most concise and yet wide-ranging discussions of time in the philosophical canon, Derrida's 1967 essay "Ousia and Grammè: A Note on a Note in Being and Time." In this text and others he publishes in the following years, Derrida will make explicit the notion of spacing at work in all aspects of his later thought, the same notion that I argue in this last chapter is at the heart of any attempt to think through the problem of interpretation.

Of Time and Spacing

The problem of what Derrida called "spacing," short for the becoming time of space and the becoming space of time, or the movement of differance itself, is profoundly related to the issues we have been discussing thus far. This is the case despite the effort that Derrida put into distancing himself from Lacan precisely insofar as Lacan's thought appeared to him to deny the movement of differance through its insistence on the fixation of an absent center to desire—the place of castration representing for Derrida an absolute reference point, the original object that, psychoanalysis's objections to the contrary, must in fact be assumed to have been there in order to have been lost or misplaced. We will have occasion in this section to return to Derrida's arguments in some detail, but our initial foray will be into the concept of spacing as derived from a psychoanalytic perspective. As we will see, spacing is at the heart of an interpretation of psychoanalysis that understands interpretation to be essential to human endeavors. According to this interpretation, spacing can be affirmed or denied, although its effects cannot be avoided, and the respective affirmation and denial of spacing correspond to different models of political agency and identity. In the following pages I will derive examples of such models from several instances of modern Latin American literary production, instances that in my mind demonstrate the operativity of spacing in models of national identity.

The problem at hand can be tentatively (and problematically) expressed, as it was in our discussion of Deleuze, in terms of the "relation" between reality and language. In Gabriel García Márquez's renowned novel *One Hundred Years of Solitude*, an episode is recounted in which the inhabitants of Macondo suffer a communal attack of insomnia. This plague (*peste*), as the narrator refers to it, manifests a certain indigenous flavor in that its host—or in this case perhaps better said its spokesperson, as the plague has fundamentally to do with language—is an Indian woman named Visitation, as in the Visitation of the angel to the Virgin, the encounter between contrary substances or realities that gives way to a new reality. This visitation, by an indigenous woman to a people whose language is the result of a colonial transplantation, brings to that people a "plague of insomnia that had flagellated her tribe for several years."[3] Such a plague, especially when described not as an inability to sleep but as a total lack of weariness, seems to us—denizens of a modernity as incapable of limiting its consumption of time as it is its consumption of goods—rather a dream than a nightmare, a cure than a plague. It seems the same at first for the citizens of Macondo, of whom we read "at first no one was alarmed. On the contrary, they were pleased not to sleep, because at that time there was so much to do in Macondo that the time barely sufficed" (García Márquez 101). That the plague is fundamentally a problem of time is revealed in a historical event that precedes the visitation of insomnia, with the departure of the birds and "the installation in their place of musical clocks in all the houses. They were beautiful clocks of handcrafted wood that the Arabs exchanged for guacamayas, and that José Arcadia Buendía synchronized with such precision that every half hour the town rejoiced in the progressive harmonies of the same tune, culminating in an exact and unanimous midday with the complete waltz" (95).

It is doubtless that the event of the installation of the clocks marks the entrance into their world of what we could recognize as modern temporality, in distinction to another temporality, perhaps ancient but in any case other, that is not measured in the regular repetitions of a synchronized sound. Perceiving the passing of time in this way relies on a synthesis of disparate experiences through the mediation of an abstract moment on which the syn-chronization depends, which in turn entails the introduction of a lack into the smooth change or caducity in which the profound experience of temporality is rooted. As the following sentence tells us: "It was also José Arcadio Buendía who decided in those years to plant the streets of the town with almond trees instead of acacias, and who discovered without ever revealing it the method for making them eternal"

(103), suggesting that the synchronization of time and the discovery of eternity are in some way related.

The loss of sleepiness, received at first as a gift, confronts the town with a temporality that its technology had tried to evacuate, that is, the unsustainable vacuity of time in its uninterrupted flow, its flowing without syncopation: "They worked so much that soon they had no more to do, and they found themselves at three in the morning with their arms crossed, counting the notes in the waltz of the clocks" (101). In the hope of recapturing their lost sleepiness, the townspeople resorted to "all sorts of methods of exhaustion . . . repeating for hours and hours the same jokes, complicating to the limits of exasperation the story of *el pollo capón*" (101). What the situation of the town suffering from the plague of insomnia presents for us, in other words, is the perverse satisfaction of the desire for the undesirable, the desire for a cessation of time, provided by the disappearance of sleepiness, which results in the pure confrontation with an unbearable temporality, a temporality as such.

It is not illogical, then, to jump from the symptom of insomnia to the greater symptom, one that provokes in the townspeople a greater fear: the symptom of forgetting. In their vain efforts to protect against the inexorable loss of memory that had been the direct effect of the plague of insomnia, José Arcadio and the townspeople develop a system of notation, beginning with the most concrete terms that have simply slipped their minds but rapidly progressing to the explicit explication of the use of things ("This is the cow, you have to milk her everyday in order to produce milk, and the milk you boil in order to mix it with coffee and make coffee with milk" [102–3]), even to the most abstract and metaphysical reminders ("God exists"): "In that way they continued to live a sifted reality, momentarily captured by words, but that was to flee irremediably when they forgot the meaning of the written letters" (103). Reality is sifting (*escurridiza*), but is its sifting nature merely the effect of a plague? That is to say, does the plague affect reality itself or only the ability of the people to capture reality through the tool of language? Or is the forgetting of the value of the letters itself merely an effect of the loss of sleepiness?

What I am proposing here is an intertwined response to all three questions: sifting is essential to reality (what Xavier Zubiri would call the essential caducity of the real)[4]; the technological time of modern temporality is one specific way of avoiding or covering this essence of reality; the indigenous visitation, the contact with a temporality other to this modern temporality, contaminates the town with a rupture in its technological syncopation of daily life, which is manifested in the first place in the inability to sleep. (This is how we must understand the original manifestation of the plague: it is a plague of contact, not brought by one people to another but generated by the contact between systems of temporality. Visitation's tribe could also not sleep, owing to their contact with a temporality foreign to their own.) The impossibility of sleeping provokes a direct (and, we should add, itself impossible) confrontation with temporality as the sifting away of reality. This confrontation presents itself for the perspective of a modern temporality based on the measurement of time through the repetition of the same—and consequently the relativizing of the changeable or sifting in the face of an implicit and unchangeable eternity—as the perverse satisfaction of that impossible desire: the cessation of technological time is equivalent to the cessation of the very distinction—or better yet to the revelation of the impossibility of the distinction—between temporality as relative change and the eternal. In pure temporality there is neither relative change nor eternity; there is only the essential caducity of the real (intrinsically unrepresentable, of course, as representation at a minimum entails some fixation or the temporal synthesis of relative change).

Yet how are we to resolve the original question of whether the plague affects reality itself or merely the ability to capture reality in language? Let us imagine again the situation in Macondo after some time spent under the conditions provoked by the plague. In order to be carried out, each series of actions constitutive of daily life would have to be made explicit in written form—not only every logical connection, not even only the implicit use of a thing, but even the definition of each word in each sentence written to explain each action, in an infinite exposition of what Heidegger called the totality of referentiality understood in each action, and therefore underlying any effort of the understanding to figure an object as something there, at hand, to be used.[5] Heidegger called this totality of references significance (*Bedeutsamkeit*) and argued that it would be incorporated implacably into any simple or pure act of perception as its condition of possibility. In order to be able to believe that reality is composed of a series of objects lying around in front of us, we have to forget or at least not be aware of the constant functioning of significance. Such forgetting is normal and perhaps universal, and it has been canonized as philosophy in the western metaphysical tradition. But not seeing the functioning of significance beneath the perception of things goes together with Dasein's incapacity to project itself on its possibilities as possibilities, which would imply living life not only as an unfinished or unfinishable project but also as a project that carries with it the possibility of its own impossibility, in other words to live one's life not as an object traveling *through* the medium of time but rather as the radical caducity of time that it in fact *is*. As Borges writes at the end of his "New Refutation of Time": "Time is the substance of which I am made. Time is a river that buffets me, but I am the river; it is a tiger who destroys me, but I am the tiger; it is a fire that consumes me, but I am the fire."[6] To arrive at that terminus, to live, in Heidegger's terminology, authentically,[7] implies in turn not merely glimpsing something like the truth hidden behind the illusions imposed by Dasein's status of having been thrown into existence and social life; rather, the truth thus revealed would be of the world in its inherent temporality, liberated from inauthentic convictions that situate change as the movement of beings against the immobile backdrop of an eternal and unchangeable reality.

If we accept this philosophical vision, or rather if we accept for the moment the potential dialogue between this vision and García Márquez's fictional plague, then we are brought to this decisive conclusion: the forgetting brought on by insomnia cannot be the result of an incapacity of language to seize a sifting reality; rather, the direct confrontation with another temporality provoked by the loss of sleep liberates the fugacity of significance, which in its essence, like Dasein and reality itself, does not have the character of an object objectively present but instead the constant falling away of temporality, caducity, forgetting. If, with the arrival in Macondo of Melquíades, normalcy returns, we should believe that this was due not to the intervention of "a substance of mild color" (García Márquez 104) but to a new technological artifice, the daguerreotype: "José Arcadio had never heard of that invention, but when he saw himself and all his family displayed for an eternity on a metal laminate the color of a sunflower, he was dumbfounded in his stupor" (105). Perhaps, in a world that does not yet know the finality of death, if we lose the protection offered to us by the syncopation of our daily lives, we take refuge in a *techne* that wrests from life a little piece of eternity, or at least suggests that.

Of what does this so-called syncopation consist? Albeit temporal, it could still be expressed by a spatial term, that is, as a certain spacing of time, a making or taking of space within time, according to which sleeping would have precisely the value of a relaxation of vigilance, of doing, of thinking. This suggests an interweaving of temporal and spatial axes, in that spacing is a *taking a distance from* that indicates as much the where of things as the when of events. Spacing does not have to be the absence of something present, and in fact it could never be, because the present can only occur by way of a more fundamental spacing, as Derrida already showed in his earliest writings,[8] the opening or clearing in the forest that Heidegger called *Lichtung*, a clearing through which the light shines.[9]

Perhaps the phenomenon we are considering has its most exemplary spatial manifestation in Borges's story "Funes el Memorioso," in which the titular character, Ireneo Funes, "is handicapped at nineteen years because of having been thrown from his horse."[10] Already known in his town as "chronometric Funes" for his ability as a child to always know the time, exactly, without consulting a watch, Funes lives the accident as a kind of end of time in his own life, from which point on he ceases to move and remains in the darkness of his room, "his eyes fixed on the fire in the back, or on a spider web" (Borges I, 486). It would seem absurd to claim that a text so obsessed with time (punctuated with references to the dates of deeds, to memories—as in the first words of the text, "I remember"—to the exact minute when something occurred) would have as its theme space. Yet the perfection of Funes's memory draws that very memory into an aporetic abyss between space and time. Since the moment (time) of his fall, Funes is paralyzed, incapable of moving in space but also incapable of forgetting (time, again). The parallels with Macondo's experience are suggestive: a medical condition (paralysis, plague) provoked by an event (fall, visitation) causes an incapacity to sleep in combination with a malfunction of memory (incapacity to remember in Macondo, incapacity to forget in Funes's case). As I sketched out in the case of Macondo, there is a close relationship between the phenomenon of insomnia and that of the loss of memory. Such a relationship also exists in Funes's case, but its directionality is inverted. Funes loses the capacity to forget, and as a result he cannot sleep; Macondo loses the capacity to sleep, and as a result it cannot remember. In the first case sleep would seem to depend on a certain ability to detach or distance oneself from an attentive and perceptive relation to lived reality, that is, what we have referred to as de-liberation. In the second case, memory would seem to depend on precisely the same de-liberation! In other words, Macondo cannot sleep, and it cannot remember, whereas Funes cannot forget and he cannot sleep. If we were to accept the equivalence that suggests itself, then we would be led to an apparently absurd conclusion: not being able to remember is the same as not being able to forget or, without the negations, remembering is forgetting. Yet the absurdity of this conclusion results only from the absoluteness of its terms, for the equation is unassailable if we assume an absolute forgetting and an absolute remembering.

The absolute loss of memory would be theoretically a total immersion in lived phenomena without the slightest representative or communicative distance, without, that is, space for interpretation. The loss of memory is thus figured in precisely the same way as a loss of language, a language that itself represents the collapse of pure particularity and the introduction of an index of universality. For this reason the townspeople of Macondo defend themselves against the onslaught of oblivion with a hyperbolic production of language, and if absolute forgetting does not arrive to Macondo, then it is only through the intervention of a reproductive technology: daguerreotype as moment of universality. From the moment the photograph takes our image, time is introduced as the ineradicable change between ourselves and that image; it is not that the photo is timeless, but rather that time as a series of nows[11] emerges when the fundamental caducity of reality, its temporality, meets with a representation or aspect of universality. This is the basis of what I have called syncopation.

What about absolute memory, or the incapacity to forget? Funes's destiny is that of a perfect memory. From the moment of his fall he forgets nothing:

Where we would perceive in a glance three cups on a table, Funes sees all the shoots and bunches and fruits that compose a grapevine. He knew the forms of the southern clouds on the morning of the thirtieth of April, 1882, and could compare them in his memory with the seams of a book of Spanish pulp that he had only seen once, and with the lines of foam raised by an oar in the Rio Negro on the vespers of the day of the Quebracho. . . . Two or three times he had reconstructed an entire day; he never doubted once, but each reconstruction had itself required an entire day. (Borges I, 488)

When the narrator visits him after having loaned him a book in Latin and a Latin dictionary for a couple of hours because Ireneo had expressed interest in learning Latin, the memorious one speaks to him in his new classical language and cites for him perfectly the "first paragraph of the twenty-fourth chapter of the seventh book of *Naturalis historia*: "ut nihil non iisdem verbis redderetur auditum" (Borges I, 487): so that nothing heard might be repeated in the same words.

We would have to understand this as Funes's slogan: there can be no repetition, not even in language, whose essential function is, of course, repetition. This is the Derridean perception concerning what he called iterability, the observation that everything new requires repetition, and each repetition carries with it some difference;[12] or, as the comic George Carlin has put it, "Say it in my own words! How in the hell am I supposed to do that if they're the same damn words everyone else uses?" But that distance, that iterability, does not function for the one who cannot avoid perceiving the difference between each iterance, for the one who cannot stand the fact that "the dog seen frontally at 3:14 should be called by the same name as the dog seen from the side at a quarter past three" (Borges I, 489). For Funes, the richness of life is so powerful that the slightest abstraction is intolerable. In Funes's language, "each word had a particular sign, a kind of mark. . . . I tried to explain to him that the rhapsody of disconnected expressions was exactly the opposite of a system of numbers. I told him that to say 365 was to say three hundreds, six tens, and five ones, an analysis that did not exist in the 'numbers' *The Black Timothy* or *meat blanket*. Funes either didn't understand me or refused to understand me" (Borges I, 489). The narrator's conclusion is inevitable: "He had learned without effort English, French, Portuguese, and Latin. I suspect, however, that he was not very capable of thinking. To think involves differences, it is to generalize, to abstract" (Borges I, 490). But memory, one could add, is a form of thought. In order to remember, one must be able to forget something. It is that absolute lack of the most minimal distance or syncopation that makes absolute memory the same as absolute forgetting. At bottom, they are one and the same: purely fantastic malfunctions of what we could call the essence of language, or spacing.

As we have seen in Lacan's study of the Schreber case, this concept of spacing is indispensable to his understanding of paranoia. To reiterate, the paranoid subject has failed to establish what Lacan called the paternal function, that is, the orientation of the signifying apparatus around some group of signifiers whose function is precisely not to signify, or to signify the absence of signification. The importance of this function resides in the flexibility it furnishes for the symbolic world. Think of one of those children's games composed of a frame filled with little square tiles that together make up an image. Obviously, the game depends on at least one tile missing, without which the other tiles would remain immobile. Deprived of that conceptual mobility, the paranoiac finds himself or herself in an isolated world, incommunicable. Therefore, although the cases here analyzed are hyperbolic and absolute examples of this malfunction, we can nonetheless define paranoid space as one whose principal tendency is toward such a malfunction of spacing.

This definition opens the door to an analysis of literary spaces that would encompass not only a philosophical questioning in the sense that I have sketched out until now but also a markedly political questioning, in that the spaces opened onto by such an analysis are also recognizably the spaces of a *polis*, an organization of people. This polis can be general or specific. We could say, for example, and with the support of other writings of García Márquez, that the phenomena of the plague, of forgetting, and of technology express the dynamic of a polis formed by the encounter between two worlds, two historical discourses, two times, two languages. As I have suggested, that the plague was the result of an indigenous visitation (the implicit oxymoron is inspired) expresses the dynamic of an encounter between heterogeneous temporalities. What would be the contribution of the theoretical framework offered by the concept of paranoid space? Basically, it provides us with a way to conceptualize the relation between an encounter and the historical representation of that encounter. An encounter consists in the opening of a new reality (albeit one that can be unimaginably destructive for previous realities). The historical discourse of one people prior to the encounter would include certain signifiers whose function is to space in the sense developed here. In the European proto-colonial world these might be signifiers of a national identity that implicitly express universal images of humanity, for example. But when such a discourse encounters people who do not fit the implicit universal images, the paternal function closes and the movement of spacing is restricted. A paranoid universe would begin to establish itself.

In his novel *I the Supreme*, the Paraguayan author Augusto Roa Bastos creates a discourse that exposes the implicitly paranoid space within the space-time presented by a national historical discourse. The structure of the novel has as its basis the supposed autobiographical intention or desire of the first president and supreme dictator of Paraguay, José Gaspar Rodríguez de Francia. For this reason, the discourse presented is entirely obsessed with questions of language and representation:

Forms disappear, words remain, only to signify the impossible. No history can be recounted. No history that is worth being recounted. But the true language has not yet been born. Animals communicate among themselves, without words, better than we, joyful at having invented words from the primal material of the chimerical. Without foundation. No relation to life.[13]

Dr. Francia despairs of the unnecessary abstraction of language, language that is for him always artificial, incapable of corresponding to reality. History must always fail, but only because words are made of a chimerical substance, a complaint that recalls Plato's critique of writing.[14] Francia desires a language like that of Funes, without the chimerical specter of abstraction, which imposes a distance between author and story; he desires a knowledge of the real and of history, or rather of history as foundation and incorporation of the nation, communicable and communicated, universal and free of the dangers of mediation, of interpretation. Of course, what transpires in Roa Bastos's novel reveals the constant impossibility of such a desire's fulfillment or, as Francia recognizes, the independence of his words from any attempt to dominate them, to make of them the universal spokespeople of a radically singular voice. This novelistic discourse, on the contrary, reveals the inevitable failure of the paranoid discourse at the historical level and the efforts of certain political tendencies to close the opening, to put an end to spacing.

In the act of dictating, as much an actualization of authorship as authority, paranoid discourse as de-spacing does not trust any method of transmission:

They cannot make stories about the Supreme Power. If they could, The Supreme would be superfluous: in literature or in reality. Who will write those books? Ignorant people like you. . . . The words of command, of authority, words above words, will be transformed into words of cleverness, of lies. Words below words. If one wants to speak about someone at any cost, then one must not only put oneself in that person's place, one must *be* that someone. (124)

It goes without saying that in the same notion of supremacy there is also the idea of singularity, of the unrepresentable, which leads to the impossibility of writing about The Supreme without making him superfluous. But that indivisibility is the property of one thing only: the signifier, which in no way means that signification cannot and does not divide itself ad infinitum but only that the operative factor of that division is precisely the function of not dividing and of not being identical to itself that is of the signifier. Yet The Supreme wants the two, absolutely exclusive things: to be indivisible and self-identical, which is to say, to be able to identify himself, to write about himself without becoming other to himself. The Supreme is nothing other than the indivisibility of the signifier, what Lacan called the master signifier. But no one, and no thing, can be that signifier, whose function is to refer to nothing, or not to refer, to be mute, to space. To take the place of this signifier, to be this signifier, would be precisely to fill its void, to impede its function of spacing, to convert the flexibility of discourse into paranoid immobility.

The Supreme recognizes, at least at first, the duplicity of the formal act of dictating—which is at the same time thinking, or remembering, or being historical:

To match the word to the sound of thought, which is never a solitary murmur, as intimate as it may be; even less so if it is the word, the thought of dictating. If the common man never talks to himself, the Supreme Dictator always talks to the others. He directs his voice ahead of himself to be heard, listened to, and obeyed. Although he seems quiet, silenced, mute, his silence is that of a command. Which means that in The Supreme there are at least two. The I can double itself into an active third person who will adequately judge our responsibility in relation to the act about which we must decide. In my days I was a good ventriloquist. Now I cannot even imitate my own voice. (111)

To dictate, but also to think, which as Borges noted implies an act of abstraction from lived reality, requires a separation of the I from an authoritative entity, from a Him who will be the place of judgment, the guarantee of an objectivity as much historical as ethical. It is the separation between the I of the statement and the I of its enunciative authority that in the arena of psychoanalytic semiotics corresponds to the function of spacing, and it is the attempt to evade that same function that determines the paranoid aspect of The Supreme's discourse.

The desire—always failed but expressed in its paradoxical glory in Borges's story—of hegemonic discourse, be it of an individual, a movement, or a people or its ostensible representatives, to reduce to a minimum the essential spacing of language is the operative ingredient in the formation of a paranoid space, a space that claims to avoid the caducity of the real, that claims to be able to extend itself without lack to the totality of what is a people, a nation, a humanity. In the Latin American literary spaces that we have analyzed, we have witnessed the limits of spacing, logical limits where, for example, absolute forgetting and absolute memory are revealed to be the same thing, as well as the limits of its own limitation where the ownmost force of spacing surges and disrupts any attempt to impose upon it the immobility of an absolutist paranoia because the desire for immobility, as with any desire, is only the fruit of its own impossibility. If it were the case that Macondo could forget everything, that Ireneo Funes could not forget anything, or that the Supreme Dictator could write the history of his own self-writing then the result would be a universe so singular, so solitary, that, in the final words of García Márquez's great novel, it would never have "a second chance on the earth."

Vulgar Time

The subject of the temporality string is obviously time and its relation to interpretation, and as we have begun this string by delving into the notion of spacing, we can do little else but follow that lead where it takes us, namely, to one of the twentieth century's most subtle thinkers on the problem of time. Despite its disingenuously understated subtitle, "A Note on a Note in *Being and Time*," Jacques Derrida's "*Ousia* and *grammè*" is an audacious and sophisticated reading, simultaneously wide-reaching and minutely detailed, of what he argues is the inescapably aporetic structure of time in metaphysics. Yet if it did only this it would have done too little, for such an argument would be confined to a critique of metaphysical thought, whereas Derrida is concerned to do much more: to show, namely, not only that the structure of metaphysical time is inescapably aporetic but also and more crucially that we are doomed to repeat that aporetic structure because there is no other time than that of metaphysics.

Ostensibly, though, it is only a note—a note, moreover, merely concerned with another note, found toward the end of Martin Heidegger's 1927 chef d'oeuvre, *Being and Time*. Heidegger famously finishes the work that would inaugurate the deconstruction of metaphysics in the service of a new, fundamental ontology by questioning whether the way to a regained understanding of being, forgotten since the advent of Greek philosophy, did not lie in a different notion of time than the one found universally in the history of metaphysics. The latter notion he termed "vulgar," and it is the business of the note, which as Derrida notes is by far the longest in *Being and Time,* to indicate the extent to which this vulgar notion inheres in the most important philosophical works since those of the ancients.

To say the least, Derrida takes exception to what could certainly be heard as an arrogant, even condescending, tone in Heidegger's choice of terms. There are not and cannot be, he writes, two times, one primordial, original, and the other vulgar and derivative; rather, "every text of metaphysics carries within itself, for example, *both* the so-called 'vulgar' concept of time *and* the resources that will be borrowed from the system of metaphysics in order to criticize that concept. And these resources are mandatory from the moment when the sign 'time'—the unity of the word and the concept, of the signifier and the signified 'time' in general, whether or not it is limited by metaphysical 'vulgarity'—begins to function in a discourse."[15] Further on, Derrida develops the objection more completely:

That perhaps there is no "vulgar concept of time." The concept of time, in all its aspects, belongs to metaphysics, and it names the domination of presence. Therefore we can only conclude that the entire system of metaphysical concepts, throughout its history, develops the so-called "vulgarity" of the concept of time (which Heidegger, doubtless, would not contest), but also that an *other* concept of time cannot be opposed to it, since time in general belongs to metaphysical conceptuality. In attempting to produce this *other* concept, one rapidly would come to see that it is constructed out of other metaphysical or ontotheological predicates. (*MP* 63)

Derrida's objection continues by further tying in Heidegger's central and, for his project, crucial distinction between vulgar, or metaphysical, and original, or primordial, time with his infamous and embattled distinction between "authentic" (*eigentliche*) and "inauthentic" (*uneigentliche*) existence: "And all the conceptual pairs of opposites which serve the destruction of ontology are ordered around one fundamental axis: that which separates the authentic from the inauthentic and, in the very last analysis, primordial from fallen temporality" (*MP* 63). The objection is figured, and perhaps rightly so, as a kind of defense of Hegel, whom Derrida sees as unfairly impugned in Heidegger's recounting of the history of time's vulgarity. Indeed, a key passage concerns Heidegger's apparent riposte to Hegel: "'Spirit' does not fall *into* time; but factical existence 'falls' as falling (*'fällt' als verfallende*) from primordial, authentic temporality (aus *der ursprünglichen, eigentlichen Zeitlichkeit*). But this 'falling' (*'Fallen'*) has its own existential possibility in a mode of temporalizing—a mode which belongs to temporality" (*SZ* 436, qtd. in *Margins* 63, translation altered).[16]

Repeating, then, a question and reproach that should not fall on deaf ears, Derrida asks, "Why determine as fall the passage from one temporality to another? And why qualify temporality as authentic—or proper (*eigentlich*)—and as inauthentic—or improper—when every ethical preoccupation has been suspended?" (*MP* 63). To say that one should not do so, that it is *improper* to do so, is something that Derrida would not say, for it is clear that for him not only is the determination of such a fall the reapparition of "at least some Platonism" in Heidegger's discourse, it is equally true that there would remain no nonmetaphysical way to think these questions, or even to point this fact out.

Heidegger's notion of vulgar time remains, however, suspect and a vindication of a metaphysical, and hence vulgar, thought that Heidegger ostensibly seeks to undermine. But on what basis are we to accept this? Much of Derrida's argument, as I have pointed out, consists of showing that Hegel, whom Heidegger has in some way dismissed under his moniker of vulgarity, had really taken the notion of time to its limits. He had, in other words, merely "articulated both more rigorously and more rigidly" the aporia of time already to be found in Aristotle and never to be had rid of since. So what, finally, is the aporia?

It is to be found already in Aristotle's *Physics*, when he asks: What is the nature of time? "Time is that which 'is not,' or which 'is barely, and scarcely'" (*MP* 39). To which Derrida says:

Now how is it to be thought that time is what is not? By giving into the obvious, that time is, that time has its essence, the *nun,* which is most often translated as instant, but which functions in Greek like our word now (*maintenant*).[17] The *nun* is the form from which time can never depart, the form in which it cannot not be given; and yet the *nun*, in a certain sense, is not. If one thinks time on the basis of the now, one must conclude that it is not. The now is given simultaneously as that which is no longer and as that which is not yet. It is what it is not, and is not what it is.[18] (*MP* 39)

Toward the end of *Being and Time* Heidegger had argued that this notion of time is predicated on a certain notion of being as presence (*Anwesen-heit*), as that which lies objectively in front of us (*vorhanden*). That present thing would change over time, and its changes would be marked on the face, if you will, of something that perdures (substance) behind those changes, like the movement of a clock's hand over its face.[19] What is "real" for Dasein is thus only the instant, the now of its present time: "*Dasein* traverses the time-span allotted to it between the two boundaries in such a way that it is 'real' only in the now that hops through the succession of nows of its 'time.' For this reason one says that *Dasein* is 'temporal.' Throughout this constant change of experience, the self maintains itself in a certain selfness" (*SZ* 373). The entire argument of *Being and Time* hinges on demonstrating that this notion of Being as substance is itself based on a confusion of Being with beings, things present in the world. A new, fundamental ontology would show such a notion of Being to be derivative, and this fundamental ontology, in the final analysis, rests on another understanding of time. In the next section we will return to Heidegger's notion of original time and his elaboration of it in his *Kant and the Problem of Metaphysics*. But for now the focus must remain on the traditional or "vulgar" notion of time and the aporia it produces.

How does this traditional notion necessarily yield Aristotle's aporia? If time is understood in terms of the changes undergone by a bedrock of presence, the present thing that changes must be thought of as *being* in a certain state at any given time and as *being* in another state at some following time. Because the thing is there, it must be in that state before it changes into its subsequent state. But if we try to point out how it is before it changes, how it is now, either it is not yet there or it is already becoming that which it will be—hence it never is what it is. Alternatively, if it is what it is long enough for us to point it out, then the instant has duration and is not subject to time. We have being or we have time, but we cannot have both, and yet what is time if there is nothing there to change?

As Derrida says, Heidegger's great advance in *Being and Time* was to readdress a question evaded by this understanding of time:

In repeating the question of Being in the transcendental horizon of time, *Being and Time* thus brings to light the omission which permitted metaphysics to believe that it could think time on the basis of a being already silently predetermined in its relation to time. If all metaphysics is engaged by this gesture, *Being and Time*, in this regard at least, constitutes a decisive step beyond or within metaphysics. The question was evaded because it was put in terms of belonging to being or nonbeing, being already determined as being-present. It is what the question evades that Heidegger puts back into play from the first part of *Being and Time* on: time, then, will be that on the basis of which the Being of beings is indicated, and not that whose possibility will be derived on the basis of a being already constituted (and in secret temporally predetermined), as a present being (of the indicative, as *Vorhandenheit*), that is, as substance or object. (*MP* 47)

Nevertheless, while on the one hand admitting this distinction between how time will be thought as opposed to how it has been thought, Derrida will on the other hand reject that Heidegger is really thinking time any differently than all those who came before him because, as he says, this other way of thinking time—"as the condition for the possibility of the appearance of beings"—is as much a part of the metaphysical tradition as the vulgar version Heidegger supposedly derides: "the originality of the Kantian breakthrough, such as it is repeated in *Kant and the Problem of Metaphysics*, transgresses the vulgar concept of time only by making explicit something hinted at in *Physics IV*. Making explicit the evaded question always and necessarily keeps to the system of what is evaded" (*MP* 50). At this point Derrida footnotes *Kant and the Problem of Metaphysics*, citing one long passage from section 32, "The Transcendental Imagination and Its Relation to Time," commenting only the following: "which shows how the pure intuition of time, such as it is described in the 'Transcendental Esthetic,' is freed from the privilege of the present and the now" (*MP* 50, n29). That time is freed from the privilege of the present and the now, however, cannot be news, because it was always a part of the aporia inherent to thinking of time to think that time is not: "Time is not (among beings). It is nothingness because it *is time, that is* a past or future now. . . . This means that if it appears that one may demonstrate that time is nothing (nonbeing), it is because one already has determined the origin and essence of no-thing as time, as nonpresent under the heading of the 'not yet' or the 'already no longer'" (*MP* 50). Heidegger's alternative, guided by the impulse to return to the question evaded by metaphysics, has therefore failed insofar as the evaded question still, according to Derrida, belongs to metaphysics as much as the tradition that has evaded it.[20]

    Nevertheless, it seems to me, this is precisely where Derrida's reading falls short, where he, in fact, fails to read. For Derrida, Heidegger wants to reveal time "as the condition for the possibility of the appearance of be-ings" and as "that on the basis of which the Being of beings is indicated." For him to do so, according to Derrida, he is concerned to show a concept of time as "freed from the privilege of the present and the now." But this is, as I will now try to show, not what Heidegger is concerned to do, at least not exclusively. That Derrida might not have noticed this is not strange, given that his entire effort is expended on reading those texts Heidegger has rele-gated to the vulgar exposition of time, and he dedicates no space to what Heidegger says about what primordial or original time might be. It is as if the very notion of such a distinction so smacks of metaphysics that it can be justifiably rejected out of hand, which makes little sense because, as Derrida and Heidegger agree, that a thought is expressed in the language of meta-physics is no good reason not to read it.

Original Time

Why, Derrida asked, "determine as fall the passage from one tempo-rality to another? And why qualify temporality as authentic—or proper (*eigentlich*)—and as authentic—or improper—when every ethical preoccu-pation has been suspended?" Heidegger declares, in a passage also quoted by Derrida, that this falling itself has "its own existential possibility in a mode of temporalizing—a mode which belongs to temporality." Dasein falls into inauthentic temporality as a matter of course. Just as we tend to think of Being in terms of things present before us, we also tend to think of time as the ticking of a second hand against a motionless clock face. But this model of time became what it is by way of a more primordial temporaliza-tion, just as our notion of space as empty and objective before us came about by way of a more primordial spatialization. Spatialization and tempo-ralization are words for how Dasein came to believe in a notion of space and time as containers: that in which objects are located and change takes place.

If philosophy's job is to ask the question of Being, however, it gets off on the wrong foot by assuming that that question can be correctly answered on the basis of things as we find them in space or as they change in time. The reason for this is that prior—in both a logical and chronological sense—to our encountering things in space, we and the things encountered form a spatial world.[21] In the same way, prior to our figuring time as the incessant change that happens to present things, we and the changing things form a temporal world, in which we relate what occurs to us and to other things with phrases like "then," "now," and "on that former occasion." The move in Heidegger's fundamental ontology, in other words, is always from an outside-in to an inside-out view of things—and this is the most consistent meaning of *eigentlich*: not "authentic" or "proper," but "of or pertaining to ownness," "viewed from its own inside." Before we can remove ourselves from time and the world in order to find such endemic philosophical problems as those relating to subjectivism and objectivity (including solipsism, idealism, truth as correspondence, and countless others), for example, we are part of time and the world—we are temporal and spatial—and time and the world are for us in such a way that those problems have not yet arisen. If falling has its own "existential possibility in a form of temporalizing," what this means is that the way Dasein comes to conceive of itself and the world according to "vulgar" temporality may be brought to light, revealed for what it is existentially, in the context of fundamental ontology.[22]

As we saw in the Aristotelian derivation of time's aporia analyzed by Derrida, the tradition has been forced when thinking about time into one or another decision, each contradictory: either the interval of time is always further divisible, in which case nothing can change because there is never a minimal *thing* to change, and hence no time; or there is a minimal interval that cannot be altered, a duration, in which case that instant is not subject to time.[23] Each of these decisions is accountable for Heidegger from a position that thinks of time as what he calls *ecstatic unity*. If Dasein is fundamentally temporal as an ecstatic unity, this means that the various disparate moments or nows that "constitute" Dasein's life are always already Dasein as a unity—there is no previous simple or unified Dasein that undergoes the experience of dispersion; conversely, any one lasting now or moment, duration, is always already ecstatic, outside itself, never present to itself— temporal. Heidegger derives this notion of duration as follows:

The "lasting" [*"Währen"*] is articulated with the awaiting and presencing understanding of the "during" [*"während"*]. This duration is again the time revealed in the *self*-interpretation of temporality, a time that is thus actually, but unthematically, understood in taking care as a "span." The making present that awaits and retains interprets a "during" as *spanned* only because in so doing it is disclosed to *itself* as the ecstatic *stretching along* of historical temporality, even though it does not know itself as this. (*SZ* 409)

In other words, Dasein stretches along as an ecstatic unity of having been that is now going to be. In relating things to itself and to others, it places certain of them as taking place "while" (*während*) something else takes place. It then interprets this "while" as a time-span or duration it moves through because, although it is disclosed to itself (*sich . . . erschlossen ist*) as a stretching along, it does not know itself as such (*als solche unerkannt*). Coming to know, thematically, what is already disclosed to oneself is the task of ontology.

As Magda King puts it in her commentary: "While the datability[24] of the 'then,' 'now,' and so forth, as we have seen, springs primarily from the *ecstatic* unity of temporality, the spannedness of the 'during' springs primarily from its ecstatic *unity*, for only the unity of a making present that awaits can make the time *between* a 'now' and a 'then' disclosable and *expressible*" (King 333). What this means is that original time will tend to be interpreted either with regard to its ecstatic dimension, as dispersion of moments or times, or with regard to its nature as a unity, in which case "spannedness" or duration comes to the fore. Dasein, far from being a simple unit moving in a temporal way along a span, is in its very constitution a having-been-that-is-now-going-to-be. Dasein is thus ecstatic, dispersed into various temporal moments, but that dispersion is equally Dasein in its only unity; that is, it is not something that a previously unified Dasein undergoes. Hence ecstatic unity—its very dispersion is its only unity.[25] By approaching Dasein from the outside, as a thing found in the world, the tradition has been forced to choose between Dasein's ecstasis, or dispersion—leading to one side of the aporia (infinite divisibility)—and its unity—leading to the other side (duration). But as Derrida so effectively demonstrates, the resulting aporia is just that: α-πορος, impossible.

At this juncture it makes sense to give an example of how philosophy might seek to avoid the aporia via the notion of duration. In his *Creative Evolution*, Henri Bergson argues that divisibility is an action of the intellect, retroactively imposed on a duration that itself is not composed of discrete instants. Nevertheless, this nondiscrete experience, which he calls duration, is in no way static; rather, it is conceived of as incessant change: "But it is expedient to disregard this uninterrupted change, and to notice it only when it becomes sufficient to impress a new attitude on the body, a new direction on the attention. Then, and then only, we find that our state has changed. The truth is that we change without ceasing, and that the state itself is nothing but change."[26] This formulation, however, still begs the questions of what is undergoing the incessant change: if some-thing, then time is negated; if no-thing, then nothing changes, and time is negated.[27] Although Deleuze has allied himself with Bergson while limiting his mentions of Heidegger as much as possible, passages such as this one from *Difference and Repetition* (a book Deleuze describes at the outset as continuing Heidegger's project—among others—of ontological difference) suggest a complex rapprochement: "If a new present were required for the past to be constituted as past, then the former present would never pass and the new one would never arrive. No present would ever pass were it not past 'at the same time' as it is present; no past would ever be constituted unless it were first constituted 'at the same time' as it was present."[28] The first part of Deleuze's formulation here repeats Aristotle's aporia in that the new present, the new *nun*, will never arrive without already being a past itself; but Deleuze's "solution" is to "expand" the present, as it were, to make it include the past and the future—a notion that is not compatible with the *nun*, which is explicitly negated by the past and the future. Whereas the Bergsonian notion of duration—incessant change prior to the divisions imposed on it by conceptual thought—would not appear to escape the aporia, Deleuze's account of the coexistence of past and present (and, of course, future) could be read as compatible with Heidegger's notion of the ecstatic unity of time.[29]

Heidegger's notion of time as ecstatic unity thus attempts to account for the aporia of time in its traditional theorization by explaining the origin of either side of the aporia. If "falling," which Derrida challenges as a description of the passage from one temporality to another, has "its own existential possibility in a mode of temporalizing—a mode which belongs to temporality," this is because the ontological understanding of temporality as ecstatic unity contains within it the "vulgar" definition and elucidates its establishment. It is therefore crucial to recognize that if we can speak of two modes of space, or two modes of time, it is not because we have these two modes available to us. As stated before, Dasein falls into inauthentic existence as a matter of course, and this falling has its own existential possibility. What Heidegger means by this—and this is why he insists, as Derrida reports, that in the project "every ethical preoccupation has been suspended"—is that the difference between authentic and inauthentic Being is a matter of ontology, not of ethics—of description and not prescription. By falling into derivative temporality and not philoso-phizing about the falling, one remains merely inauthentic—that is, one continues to philosophize from an outside perspective; but authenticity does not mean not falling. Rather, it means falling and philosophizing about falling; it means nothing other than distinguishing between primor-dial and derivative time and telling the story of why Dasein falls.

To begin with, then, having described the falling, how do we now describe primordial temporality? Not a point that moves along a line, or a series of nows that endlessly succeed one another—both of which repre-sent the outside-in (*uneigentlich*) view of time—primordial temporality—temporality described from within Dasein (*eigentlich*)[30]—consists of what Heidegger characterizes as *Erstreckung*, or stretching along, a having been that is also and inseparably a now and a going-to-be: "The ontological clar-ification of the 'connectedness of life,' that is, of the specific way of stretching along, movedness (*Bewegtheit*) and persistence of Dasein, must accordingly be approached in the horizon of the temporal constitution of this being. The movedness of existence is not the motion of something ob-jectively present. It is determined from the stretching along of Dasein" (*SZ* 374–75). Existence is certainly in constant motion, or subject to con-stant change, but we should not confuse this with the motion of an object moving in a separable environment. Rather, Dasein is its own being moved, or "movedness" (*Bewegtheit*), in the movement of its temporal stretching along.[31] As we have already discussed, Dasein's stretching along always refers itself and things to notes such as "then," "now," and "on that former occa-sion," and it is this "datability" of its experience that produces the "ecstasies" of past, present, and future. These are ecstasies because they are always out-side themselves, as with the *nun*. But whereas the *nun* always therefore refers to something other than now (a past or a future, for example), tem-porality as the unity of the ecstasies has no other *thing* to refer to: "*Tempo-rality is the original 'outside of itself' in and for itself*. Thus we call these characterized phenomena of future, having been, and present, the *ecstasies* of temporality. Temporality is not, prior to this, a being that first emerges from *itself*; its essence is temporalization in the unity of the *ecstasies*" (*SZ* 329). From an inside-out perspective, temporality is revealed to be origi-nally ecstatic, outside of itself, but is revealed to be so *in and for itself*—there is no absolute other to refer to, no bedrock against which to move; rather, alterity is always already part of oneself.[32]

The notion of the unity of the ecstasies is precisely chosen as a way of thinking through primordial time with Kant, who posed in perhaps its greatest detail the aporetic structure of time when he described the problem of knowledge in terms of a series of syntheses that would have to take place in order for something apprehended in the sensual manifold of space and time to be unified under a concept and hence cognized as an object. At the most basic level, a synthesis would have to take place in order for even the apprehension of a thing before us to occur, because otherwise that thing would, at the level of bare perception, be nothing other than a temporal succession of unconnected impressions. Kant describes three modes of synthesis as forming the basis of this function, and it is in *Kant and the Problem of Metaphysics*, and in fact in the section from which Derrida quotes without fully reading, that Heidegger reads these passages from Kant in the service of his most thoroughgoing examination of time. This reading offers, in my view, the best explanation of how primordial time must differ from derivative time and of why making this distinction should not be avoided on the grounds that it repeats certain metaphysical gestures.

For Kant, the imagination is the faculty situated "between" sensibility and the understanding and has the job of mediating between the two. For Heidegger, the imagination, insofar as it is fundamental to knowing, has a crucial relation to time:

Pure imagining, however, which is called pure because it forms its fabric [*Gebilde*] out of itself, as in itself relative to time, must first of all form time. Time as pure intuition means neither just what is intuited in pure intuiting nor just the intuiting which lacks the "object." Time as pure intuition is the forming intuiting of what it intuits *in one*. This gives the full concept of time for the first time.

Pure intuition, however, can only form the pure succession of the sequence of nows as such if in itself it is a likeness-forming, prefiguring, and reproducing power of imagination. Hence, it is no way permissible to think of time, especially in the Kantian sense, as an arbitrary field which the power of imagination just gets into for purposes of its own activity, so to speak. Accordingly, time must indeed be taken as pure sequence of nows in the horizon within which we "reckon with time." This sequence of nows, however, is in no way time in its originality. On the contrary, the transcendental power of the imagination allows time as [a] sequence of nows to spring forth, and as this letting-spring-forth it is therefore original time.[33]

For Heidegger the pure imagination is the fulcrum of knowledge, the meeting point of sense and understanding, and in this position its primary task is the formation of time as pure intuiting. To understand the strangeness and at the same time normalcy of this move, one must see it in the context of Heidegger's consistent strategy in reading Kant, of demonstrating that wherever Kant begins with what would seem to be separate faculties that then converge upon a particular function, in fact it can only make sense to locate the analysis of a pre-existing, albeit ecstatic, unity—for example, the imagination does not "find" time already there as the form of intuition, as it were, but rather must form time out of itself. Taken at face value, then, the imagination would have the function of synthesizing, through the agency of what Kant calls schemata, the jumbled diversity of sensible intuitions in their temporal and spatial manifold under stable and unchanging concepts. Without this function, of course, knowledge could never take place: the jumble of spatial and temporal intuitions comprising the experience of a dog, for example, could never be unified under the concept "dog" that allows for the object "dog" to be cognized.[34] Time, the fundamental form of inner intuition, would intervene preventing even a relatively unchanging set of intuitions to coalesce. But in Heidegger's reading, time is not an element of intuition abstracted from its content and its eventual synthesis in the imagination; rather, the imagination forms time in the very act of synthesis. This in no way means that there is a "moment" in which the imagination is not already temporal; the opposite, rather, is the case. What Heidegger means is that no one faculty can ever be atemporal, as no faculty precedes the synthesis in which time is formed.

There are, for Kant, three kinds of synthesis: the synthesis of apprehension in intuition, the synthesis of reproduction in imagination, and the synthesis of recognition in concepts. According to Heidegger's reading, the modes of temporality that constitute "the threefold unity of time as present, having been, and future" (*KPM* 124) are already contained within these three kinds of synthesis. In this way Heidegger understands the synthesis of apprehension in intuition, by which something is apprehended at all, as constitutive of the now; the synthesis of reproduction in imagination, by which the mind retains previous impressions, as constitutive of having-been; and the synthesis of recognition in concepts, by which the mind "holds the being before us as one which is the same" (*KPM* 130), as constitutive of the future. To put it as succinctly as possible, Kant posits three kinds of synthesis as the minimal requirement for intuitions in time and space to be unified under concepts and become cognitions, but Heidegger argues that it is from the three syntheses themselves that time as a series of nows flowing from the past into a future springs forth and that it is the transcendental power of the imagination as the seat of these syntheses that must be conceived of as original time.

If Heidegger has shown that the imagination forms time as pure intuition, then it only remains to be seen what the relation is between that unity (imagination and sensibility) and the faculty of the understanding. For Kant, the concept or understanding has to be brought into unity with sensibility because whereas the latter is intuited in the form of a manifold—space as exteriority and time as succession—the former responded only to the law of non-contraction or identity. At the core of the reasoning mind is the transcendental apperception, the mere thought of "I" that accompanies all other thoughts and acts as a kind of anchor that unifies the field of concepts, that makes them belong to one and the same consciousness. For Heidegger's reading of Kant, however, transcendental apperception can no longer be conceived of as separate from time because it has been discovered in the unity of the other two faculties: "In this way, however, it is obvious at a glance that time as pure self-affection is not found 'in the mind' 'along with' pure apperception. Rather, as the ground for the possibility of selfhood, time already lies within pure apperception, and so it first makes the mind into a mind" (*KPM* 134). If pure apperception is also temporal, Heidegger reasons, then this explains the otherwise strange comparison Kant makes between time and the I, when he says on the one hand that "the fixed and perduring I (of pure apperception) constitutes the correlate of all of our representations" (*KPM* 134) and on the other that time is that which in change "perdures and does not change" (*KPM* 134):

This "fixing" and this "perduring" are no ontic assertions concerning the unchangeability of the I, but are transcendental determinations which mean the following: insofar as the I as such brings before itself in advance something like fixedness and perduring in general, it forms the horizon of selfhood within which what is objective becomes experienceable as the same throughout change. The "fixed" I is so called because as "I think," i.e., as "I place before," it brings before itself [something] like standing and enduring." (*KPM* 135)

If Kant refers time and time again to the principle of noncontradiction as atemporal, or to pure apperception as not being subject to temporal form, this is, for Heidegger, perfectly understandable, for Kant is oriented toward the non-original essence of time. Understood in its original form, however, time inheres even in the principle of noncontradiction, that is, that A cannot be *at the same time* A and not A: "Rather, the 'at the same time' expresses that temporal character which as preliminary 'recognition' ('pre-paration') originally belongs to all identification as such" (*KPM* 136). That is to say, the concept is in some ways the essence of original temporality, because by bringing "before itself in advance something like fixedness and perduring in general, it forms the horizon of selfhood within which what is objective becomes experienceable as the same throughout change." At the same time, the concept in its unity with intuition and imagination is what lets time as a sequence of nows, hence vulgar, derivative time, spring forth. Original time, in other words, is not a state that we ever inhabit or can ever return to, and in this sense its description does not run afoul of the "quest for an *archia* in general" that Derrida calls the " 'essential' operation of metaphysics" (*MP* 63). Rather, it is only the orientation according to which we speak of time as either being fundamentally, from the ground up, experienced externally, outside of ownness (*uneigentlich*) or as being experienced externally only by way of a diversion, a falling, a springing forth whose dominant rule inscribes the blind spot of its own becoming. Vulgar time, in other words, is the concept for time that is disclosed to itself as temporal but is philosophically unaware of that disclosure; it is a concept in the grip of an illusion.

Memorious Time

Now let us speak more plainly. Original time is not prehistoric; it is not how things once were in a purer, less vulgar time; as Heidegger emphasizes, "*The vulgar representation of time has its natural reason*" (*Die vulgäre Zeitvorstellung hat ihr natürliches Recht*) (*SZ* 426). We all tend to understand time according to its vulgar representation because our sensory experience is "spaced" by the concept, the most profound, or at least constant, of which is the I.[35] What makes this now another than the now before it is, of course, the designator "now," just as what allows for changes in time and kind among, for example, dogs, is the designation of the concept "dog." One result of the use of concepts is physical ontology and vulgar time; it is vulgar because we all do it. All fundamental ontology wants is to show how it is produced and to ensure that the illusions of permanence and presence necessitated by it not be turned into philosophical or even theological monuments. That said, the debate I have staged here may appear irresolvable: who is to say that Heidegger got it right in positing the difference between vulgar and original time? Alternatively, who is to say that Derrida's assertion that there can be only one concept of time is justified? It may be that Funes has the answer.

Recall that in Borges's story Ireneo Funes is thrown from his horse at the age of nineteen and for the next and last two years of his life is incapable of forgetting anything: "he not only remembered every leaf of every tree of every hill, but also every one of the times he had perceived or imagined it" (Borges I, 489). One result of this new experience of the world is that differences that used to be passed over with equanimity become annoyingly evident, such that "his own face in the mirror, his own hands, surprised him each time" (Borges I, 489). This annoyance spreads to language, and he finds it increasingly intolerable that he must use a single word to name what for him are such strikingly different phenomena: "Not only did it tax him to understand that the generic symbol *dog* should comprise so many disparate individuals of diverse sizes and shapes; it irritated him that the dog seen frontally at 3:14 should be called by the same name as the dog seen from the side at a quarter past three" (Borges I, 489). What we should notice here is that Borges has established a clear connection between remembering things from the past and noticing differences, both spatial and temporal. Insofar as Funes notices a difference, he wants a different word for it. Indeed, as the narrator informs us, what Funes would like is a language Locke once speculated about but cast off as being too particular. A language with a word for every thing, said Locke, would not be a language because it would lack the necessary generality needed to communicate.[36] For Funes, on the contrary, it would be far too general, as it would not be able to distinguish all the changes things undergo or even the same things at different moments. But Funes can, apparently.

Borges often likes to play with different kinds of impossibility.[37] His Pierre Menard famously turns up his nose at *becoming* a seventeenth-century Spaniard in order to reproduce word for word the *Quijote*. This impossible task was not impossible enough for his ambition, which wanted to conquer the task from the seat of a subject living in a different culture, in a different time, and with radically different experiences. In the same way, Funes's dismissal of Locke's language as too general should provoke our laughter, for it pushes to its uttermost absurdity the very notion of thought Funes is said to be gifted with.

To think, as Borges writes, "is to forget differences, to generalize, to abstract" (Borges I, 490). One needs to be able to forget or at least overlook the differences between species in order to have the concept of a genus. Funes apparently cannot forget, but he must be able to ignore, to overlook. He must, in other words, be able to have a concept of dog that spans all the species and all those states and all those times, in order to know enough to be "irritated" at the generality of "dog." In the same way, Funes must have a concept of himself, of his face and his hands, for instance, that transcends the manifold of ways and times they are presented to him, in order to be "surprised" by that manifold. Yet to have these concepts Funes must, at least at times, at least in part, be able to forget the difference they unify.

In Borges's story, Funes represents what for Kant would be the manifold of intuition without or prior to synthesis by the imagination and unification under a concept. To take the most basic level of inner intuition, Funes's experience of a dog in front of him, even one that remained still, would be an irresolvable succession of sensory input, incapable of coalescing into the object "dog." Yet Funes, who can think the inadequacy of the signifier and be irritated at its generality, is clearly synthesizing. Insofar as he can have, in fact, a subjective experience of manifold, he must have a minimum capacity to synthesize, that is, to tell apart the temporal moments that constitute that manifold.[38] To quote a sentence from Heidegger that easily could have been written about Funes, "It is easily seen that the pure intuition of the pure succession of nows cannot be the taking-in-stride of a presence [*Anwesenden*]. If it were, then at most it would be able to 'intuit' just the current now, and never the sequence of nows as such and the horizon formed in it. Indeed, strictly speaking, in the mere taking in stride of a present 'moment' [*eines 'Gegenwärtigen'*] it is not possible to intuit a single now insofar as it has an essentially continuous extension in its having-just-arrived and its coming-at-any-moment" (*KPM* 122). It cannot be the case, in other words, that time as a succession of nows (the *nun*) is "encountered" in the form of intuition. If that were the case, there would not even be the merest perception of succession and hence need for synthesis, for the perceiving subject would only ever perceive the now and never its succession. In the same way, we can say of Funes's experience that, were his intuition really without a concept and hence without abstraction or overlooking, his pure intuiting would never be more than a current now, and he would not even have the "horizon" to realize that something like time was taking place. The problem of manifold and its synthesis, in other words, requires that temporality as ecstasis be always already a kind of a unity; dispersion without unity would never register as dispersion in the first place.

Yet the opposite is also true, in a move that distances Borges, Derrida, and Heidegger from a more classical phenomenology of time consciousness, like that of Husserl.[39] The idea of the unity of past, present, and future in the fleeting of the now is insufficient to grasp the aporetic nature of time, which is irreducibly ecstatic and never present to itself. Memorious time, then, must be understood as always external to itself, cloven by difference at the heart of its most intimate self presence. Funes is *necessarily* in contradiction with himself, for he cannot at once synthesize and experience reality in a saturated way. To put it in another way, the immediate saturation of reality is simultaneously permitted and negated by the ecstatic synthesis of time. This is also the key to Borges's life-long obsession with time, a philosophical problem that for him found its truest expression in Zeno's paradox of Achilles and the tortoise, whereby the swift Achilles is condemned to lag behind the ponderous tortoise for all eternity given that the space separating them is infinitely divisible. The paradox of divisibility, Borges concludes, "is incontestable, unless we confess the ideality of space and time."[40] Others have taken this to be the proof of Borges's ultimate Platonism: "The component of Platonism that persists in Borges is at every moment the model one: the key to the world is outside of it, in another world."[41] But in my mind this is a complete misconstrual. That Borges insists on the ideality of space and time means that he insists on the difference between knowledge and known, the suspension from reality of the gaze, the razor's edge of perception, if you will, but not on its location in a timeless world. If Borges attributes the error in the emergence of the idealist objects of Tlön in our world to the failure to distinguish between a "rigor of chess masters" and a "rigor of angels,"[42] the latter would be precisely characterized by its unavailability, by the fact that something must escape our grasp.

This insistence on ideality may be an explicit Kantianism on Borges's part, but if it is, it is a Kantianism more in line with Heidegger's Kant, one that reads in the necessary irreducibility of the phenomenon not a positive ghost world of permanent if ineffable forms but the persistent irruption of difference that produces the specter of the real. The ideality of space and time, then, is nothing other than the effect of spacing, the way reality seems to shed its leaves like a book as we exhaustively search it for a symbolic truth. For this is the ineluctable paradox that Borges's fiction never tires of exploring, the paradox of the philosopher's desire: that the search for a symbolic truth in an imaginary reality yields a phantom object whose promised fulfillment will never be paid "until the return of the stone guest I shall be for you since you call me forth."[43]

What Funes as thought-experiment demonstrates, therefore, is that there can be no notion of time or of temporal succession that does not always already presuppose synthesis and concept and no notion of synthesis or unity that does not already presuppose difference or ecstasy—which is another way of saying that time is spacing and that spacing is the work of the signifier. We all, Funes included, experience the flow of time only because our experience of having been, of now, and of not-yet-here is originally formed, spaced, by our use of the concept. Yet it is our use of the concept that guides us just as surely to another concept of time, one based on presence as substance that the concept engenders as the essence of all things. According to this concept, time is nothing but a succession of nows, of moments ticking off against the face of an immobile being. According to this concept, there is and can be no other way of thinking time, and the aporias that result from it are as inescapable as that concept of time is to our thought. But when philosophy, taking its cue from the Hegelian directive to think itself thinking, looks back at the path this thought has taken, it will not think the path of time in a different way from how it has been thought in the tradition; rather, it will think its own thinking of that path in a different way. This, it seems to me, is what Heidegger has done and what Borges has allowed us to see.

Many years after having published his critique of Heidegger's note, Derrida returned to the fundamental issue of "*Ousia* and *grammè*" in *Aporias*, a text in which he pursues the question of a possible distinction between the authentic and inauthentic in one's relation to death. As he writes in that text:

> If death, the most proper possibility of Dasein, is the possibility of impossibility, death becomes the most improper possibility and most ex-propriating, the most inauthenticating one. From the most originary inside of its possibility, the proper of Dasein becomes from then on contaminated, parasited, and divided by the most improper. . . . These distinctions [such as that between authenticity and inauthenticity] are threatened in their very principle, and, in truth, they remain impracticable as soon as one admits that an ultimate possibility is nothing other than the possibility of an impossibility and that the *Enteignis* always inhabits the *Eigentlichkeit* before even being named there—indeed this will happen later.[44]

The bone of contention, then, would still appear to be the determination, as Derrida had earlier put it, of the passage from one temporality to another as a fall from authenticity to inauthenticity, when the authentic, the proper, the ownmost, has never not been contaminated by the term of its negation. Indeed this contamination can only result in the impossibility of the distinctions themselves (which are "threatened in their principle" and "remain impracticable"), a claim already made in the closing pages of "*Ousia* and *grammè*": "It is thus that the difference between Being and beings, the very thing that would have been 'forgotten' in the determination of Being as presence, and of presence as present, this difference is so buried that there is no longer any trace of it" (*MP* 65). Yet there is a slight difference between these claims. On the one hand, the contamination of authenticity by the inauthentic renders use of the distinction impracticable; on the other hand, the ontological difference—the unconcealment of which depends on the distinction—"is so buried that there is no longer any trace of it." But if it is buried, it is there; in fact, its burial, its erasure, is a trace in itself: "But at the same time, this erasure of the trace must have been traced in the metaphysical text. Presence, then, far from being, as is commonly thought, what the sign signifies, what a trace refers to, presence, then, is the trace of the trace, the trace of the erasure of the trace" (*MP* 66). Now if the contamination of the authentic by the inauthentic, which makes the distinction impracticable, is another name for the erasure of ontological difference, a trace of this erasure nevertheless remains, and its reading entails a practice. Furthermore, the very contamination that Derrida says inhabits *Eigentlichkeit* before being named there, what is this if not the very falling that, as Heidegger says, has its own existential possibility in a mode of temporalizing—namely, the very ontological perspective that reads the trace, the falling, and refuses to accept time as the series of nows as the foundation of all experience?

I have insisted in this discussion on emphasizing the "inside-out" connotation of *eigentlich* as opposed to the connotations of authenticity and propriety that have traditionally been emphasized and that are at the heart of Derrida's reading. In falling, the inside-out perspective is ex-propriated by the outside-in perspective of the they (*das Man*) and public time is established. But what the inside-out perspective describes is not something proper or authentic, only later to be lost or ex-propriated; what it shows, rather, is ecstatic unity, something that, as constitutive temporality, is never what it is but always what it has been and will have been. This stretching along, however, does not merely replace one presence with another one, a point with a rubber band, as it were.[45] Neither does it obliterate negativity or forgetting, as if Dasein were something integral stretched from its beginning to its end. Rather, Dasein's totality, its unity, is nothing other than the inclusion in itself of its constitutive nothingness, its gaps, its death, its throwness, its oblivion—its own impossibility as possibility. It is nothing other than the fact that there is nothing else to ground it than the not that it always also is: "Yet the time that has gaps in it does not go to pieces in this lack of togetherness, but is a mode of temporality that is always already disclosed and ecstatically *stretched out*" (*SZ* 409–10).

Hägglund describes the logic of the trace in the following words: "Even the most intimate auto-affection can only take place through the violent passage of time, which requires the spatialization of traces in order to be marked as such but also risks deleting these traces in the concomitant movement of temporalization. To think the spacing of time is thus to think how death, discrimination and obliteration are at work from the beginning and do not overtake an already constituted subject." The point I am making is that Heidegger's notion of the ecstatic unity of temporality as the essence of Dasein is in no way opposed to this notion of the trace. What Derrida is describing with this notion is time viewed from an ontological, "authentic," inside-out perspective, which he has nevertheless derived from the aporetic structure of time as viewed from an outside-in, "inauthentic," perspective. One can indeed, therefore, deny that there are two times, but not that there are two concepts of time, for the work of deconstruction (the work, if you will, of reading the deconstruction already at work in the text of metaphysics) itself depends on this distinction. It depends on, in the words of Martin Hägglund's eponymous essay, "the necessity of discrimination" between a philosophy, like Lévinas's, that invokes "an absolute that reinstates [the] ideals" of "identity, totality, and monadic being," and one like Derrida's that refuses that invocation. Does not Heidegger also, painfully at times, appear to invoke the same ideals? Certainly a current of interpretation would seem to suggest so. But what I have been concerned to demonstrate in this chapter is that this current cannot be getting it right, for to read *Eigentlichkeit* as denoting a self-same core of identity risks misunderstanding Heidegger's entire contribution to philosophy.

Why, then, does he use a language so fertile for misinterpretation? Why this apparent duplicity? Because, I have argued, he must indicate the necessity of discrimination, the distinction between the philosophy that reads the trace as trace, as constitutive temporality and ecstatic unity, and the one that reads it as the passage of time from presence to presence. When we think the trace, or the constitutive temporality of being, we bring our own "birth," itself "returned from the unsurpassable possibility of death, into existence, so that it may freely, more free from illusion, accept only the thrownness of its own There" (*SZ* 391). What Heidegger's position entails, then, is an understanding of the power of a philosophical illusion and the need to overcome it.

Epilogue: The Sense of Certainties to Come

Over the course of this book I have examined a series of textual practices that identify themselves as psychoanalytic and that are commonly identified as somehow defining the canon of psychoanalytic thought, texts that furthermore thematize in some way the issue of interpretation, in relation to two broadly ranging critiques of that thought precisely as it pertains to the issue of interpretation. Moreover, I have argued that these very critiques must themselves be seen as interpretations of psychoanalytic thought in the very sense of the concept, interpretation, that I have tried to develop out of the reading of these psychoanalytic texts. In other words, psychoanalysis, when it is read, when it is interpreted, grows, changes, becomes something new, and such change and growth are not only salubrious, they are part and parcel of the psychoanalytic practice of interpretation as such.

There might seem, at the outset, to be something violent about this trope, in that it would appear to appropriate even those discourses that try to distance themselves from psychoanalysis as themselves psychoanalytic, in a kind of abyssal game of one-upmanship. Yet my desire is not to rescue a practice from its past or redeem it from its sins as much as to recognize that to grant the critical reading its distance is not only to posit a kind of identity independent of its critical object but also, and unforgivably, to concede that psychoanalysis was just *that* and continues to be just *that* in blissful disregard of those who read it. Psychoanalysis is not an object. It is a series of practices related by what Wittgenstein called family resemblances.[1] A reading, a description, a redescription—all of these are performative on their object, and it is this performativity that I have called interpretation. Psychoanalysis only lives as long as it is being interpreted, and if these interpretations are critical, it can do nothing but benefit from them, for the furthest thing from critique is dismissal.

But these remarks are quite general, and another issue altogether is that of the extent to which the specific criticisms or interpretations of Deleuze and Guattari on the one hand and Derrida on the other substantially clash with interpretations already underway within the institutionally identifiable discourse of psychoanalysis in general and specifically in the writings and lecture of Lacan. It is perhaps unfortunate that so much time seems unavoidably to slide into debating whether the canonical text can be read only as the critic reads it or whether it too supports a more sympathetic reading, because the upshot of such a debate would seem to be that both parties debating in fact agree as to what the truth is and only disagree as to whether some earlier thinker actually thought that or in fact thought something other than that. Yet the potential of precisely such a debate is what the essential interpretability of the canonical texts reveals.

So, while I have, especially in the case of Derrida, strenuously rejected his interpretation of certain of Lacan's and Heidegger's texts, at this time what I would like to stress is a kind of implicit accord, as regards both critiques, around something I will enunciate as the truth, because I believe that to philosophize without reference to the truth is to speak as if from the place of truth.[2] The critical interpretations at issue are the following: first, does psychoanalysis repeat and re-inscribe a return to a lost fulfillment as the fundamental template of desire, and if so, is this true? If not, how can it be altered? Second, does psychoanalysis necessarily and prescriptively reterritorialize the unconscious by its insistence on the Oedipal structure of desire? Is Oedipus true, and if not, how can it be altered?

In order to return to each of these critical interpretations in turn, I will take one final pass through a third problem that has accompanied my thinking on these issues, namely, the problem of the relation between language and reality. At the risk of some repetition of my position, let me try to be as clear as possible. Talk of nondiscursive objects and talk of linguistic constructivism make me a little queasy, and they make me queasy for exactly the same reason. Whether one speaks of the social construction of reality or insists on the materiality of the world and hence its resistance to linguistic construction, one is implicitly reiterating a representational view of the world, canonical in modern philosophy, in which there exists on the one hand a world independent of the conceptual frameworks within which we receive it and on the other some conceptual framework.[3] So-called realists or materialists put their emphasis on the former and idealists or constructivists on the latter, but it makes more sense, it seems to me, to question the basic division itself. The position I support claims that the notion of real materiality devoid of its sensory interpretation or conceptual embeddedness is exactly as idealistic as the notion of a solipsistic dreamer afloat in a world of his own creation. Yet this is under no circumstances the same as denying the existence of the world or the power of thought, culture, or what have you. It is rather to say that "the existence of the world independent of thought" and "the power of thought over the dumb materiality of the world" are mere abstractions, which is another way of saying that they are symbolic utterances that we seem to want to render in an imaginary way.

If I can encapsulate an overall thesis of this book in a few lines, I would say that the thought of Lacan, of Derrida, of Deleuze and Guattari, as regards what I have been calling interpretation, constitute different facets of an attempt to do philosophy in an intellectual world born of the dismissal of the constructivism/materialism non-debate. If this is the case, we could venture the following about these different facets: Derrida tells us how to do such a philosophy, Lacan tells us why we do such a philosophy, and Deleuze simply does such a philosophy. Derrida is concerned with *how* because it is how philosophers read that concerns him and how they manage again and again to reconstitute a philosophical model of truth whose payoff is the return to something that was lost, be it a garden of Eden or that real materiality banished by the conceptual framework of a thinking being. Lacan is concerned with *why* we do such a philosophy because, in Derrida's estimation, his interest, insofar as it is philosophical, is in the philosopher's desire, a desire he describes as being oriented by the illusion that one can find in the imaginary some place of non-partition or, which is the same thing, that one can find in the symbolic an element that refers purely, immediately, to itself, the philosopher's stone, truth as self-identity. Finally, Deleuze and Guattari can be said *to do* such a philosophy precisely because they no longer thematize either the method (or the epistemology, that is, how one knows) or the desire (or the ethics, that is, why one tries to know), but rather proceed to the act of philosophizing (or ontology, just doing it), the act they describe as the creation of concepts and hence of the transformation[4] or what I would call the interpretation of the world.

It should be clear in such a model that the notion of the resistance of the world to its endless interpretation, or the notion of nondiscursive objects, can be discussed only to the extent that such categories are not understood as reverting to the metaphysical model of world versus conceptual schema. Gumbrecht's notion of presence effects against meaning effects[5] does not (or does not have to) play into this schema because the spectrum between meaning production and what he calls silence, or the absence of meaning production that corresponds to presence, is precisely a spectrum of experience that is, needless to say, always and everywhere inseparable from and unthinkable outside a culturally and historically specific context. In the same way, when Foucault poses to himself the realist objection to his project toward the end of volume I of the *History of Sexuality*, the objection that for his study of sexuality "there remain only groundless effects, ramifications without roots, a sexuality without a sex," Foucault's response is unequivocal:

far from the body having to be effaced, what is needed is to make it visible through an analysis in which the biological and the historical are not consecutive to one another, as in the evolutionism of the first sociologists, but are bound together in an increasingly complex fashion in accordance with the development of the modern technologies of power that take life as their objective. . . . Now it is precisely this idea of sex *in itself* that we cannot accept without examination. Is "sex" really the anchorage point that supports the manifestations of sexuality, or is it not rather a complex idea that was formed inside the deployment of sexuality?[6]

As an aside, it is worth noting that this passage previews, in a nutshell, exactly the argument that Judith Butler advances in her *Bodies That Matter*, in which she describes the materiality of the body as the sedimentation of a process of materialization itself inseparable from techniques of power or discursive practices, which can be productive of bodies whether they are thematizing them or excluding them, just as meaning can be silent.[7]

Given this ground of relationality among these three theoretical currents, the conclusions to this narrative, as provisional as any interpretive conclusion can be, must take the form of a brief exposition of how these critical appropriations can be understood to have themselves interpreted and hence transformed psychoanalytic thinking. In the case of Deleuze and Guattari's work, the thesis is apparent from the very title of the first book they published on the topic. The core of their interpretation is the centrality of the Oedipal triangle to the interpretive practices of canonical psychoanalytic texts, whose effect is, in their view, invariably to reterritorialize the deterritorializations of the unconscious by making desire dependent on an original fantasy, whose basic form involves the threat of castration imposed by a father over a child whose natural object of desire is the mother's body. By appropriating the concept of the unconscious as the ultimate substrate of deterritorialization, Deleuze and Guattari argue convincingly that the concept of desire as conditioned by the lack imposed by castration not only deprives the concept of the unconscious of its philosophical potential but also and more critically itself functions as an implicit reterritorialization of the powers of the unconscious. Rather than libido and repression leading to lack and its orientation of desire, they argue for desire as a spectrum spanning from production to non-production, high intensity to total entropy, a sort of fluid mechanics (itself not far from Freud's metapsychological speculations) of flows interspersed by cuts and blockages. The result of this interpretation is not a renunciation of interpretation but a correction of a problematic tendency in psychoanalysis toward the normalization of subjects; a psychoanalytic discourse that fully incorporated these corrections would no longer act under the spell of an original meaning that the analysis seeks to uncover but would rather eschew such a search in favor of the opening of a space for the various productions of the unconscious.[8] Such a renewed psychoanalysis would moreover eventually cease altogether to speak of fathers and phalluses and seek a more nuanced vocabulary that stresses the notion of a minimal distance from imaginary embeddedness and fallacious imaginary stand-ins for that which does not submit to partition.

In the case of Derrida's interpretation, what is at stake is the notion that in Lacan's analysis of philosophical desire, for which Derrida praises him, there remains inscribed and reiterated the very heart of the metaphysical device—by which the drive of analysis is ultimately limited by a resistance that takes the form of an end to analysis—a fundamental fantasy of some lost plenitude inscribed in the knowing subject as a lack or a loss to which one must return: "What is put in question by [deconstruction's] work is not only the possibility of recapturing the originary but the desire to do so or the phantasm of doing so, the desire to rejoin the simple, whatever that may be, or the phantasm of such a reunion."[9] In the place of any such phantasm, according to Derrida, "at the heart of the present, at the origin of presence, the trace, writing, or the mark is a movement of referral to the other, to otherness, a reference as difference that would resemble an *a priori* synthesis if it were of the order of judgment and if it were thetic. But in a pre-thetic and prejudicative order, the trace is indeed an irreducible binding" (*R* 27–28). To the extent that this interpretation of the analysis of desire and of psychoanalysis's desire contributes a corrective to psychoanalysis, I would venture to say that the trace (or deconstruction, dissemination, differance, etc., as Derrida lists them) is a better (more subtle, more self-aware) version of what the letter or the signifier is in Lacan's Seminar. Indeed, an adequate reading of that Seminar, as I have argued, would locate at the heart of imaginary experience experienced as a lived present the letter as an inevitable movement of referral to the other. In the very action of referral (binding) and hence of being at-least-two, the letter remains itself irreducible to any one element; it does not admit of partition and, hence, never permits the imaginary to be inhabited as presence.

Although deconstruction puts in question even the desire to recapture the originary, or the phantasm of that recapture, and hence must be seen as putting psychoanalysis itself in question, Derrida also recognizes, in his use of the term *double bind*, that "to analyze such a desire does not mean to renounce its law and to suspend the order of reason, of meaning, of the question of the origin, of the social bond" (*R* 36). There is a way in which, in other words, deconstruction must simultaneously insist on the nullity of even the phantasm of plenitude, to give it one name, and take those very phantasms "into account, so as to render an account of [them]" (*R* 36). This negated phantasm, as he admits, haunts the very heart of deconstruction itself:

What *drives* [*pousse*] deconstruction to analyze without respite the analysistic and dialecticistic presuppositions of these philosophies, and no doubt of philosophy itself, what resembles there the drive and pulse of its own movement, a rhythmic compulsion to track the desire for simple and self-present originarity, well, this very thing—here is the double bind we were talking about a moment ago—drives it to raise the analysistic and transcendentalistic stakes. . . . In this sense, deconstruction is also the interminable drama of analysis. (*R* 29)

To drive, *pousser*, is emphasized as a clear analogue to Lacan's *pulsion*, that drive that he theorizes apart from desire, starting in the early 1960s as being the fundamental corruption of signification,[10] a movement or slippage untamed by imaginary objects or promises of fulfillment, auto-affection insofar as that affection corresponds to the radical inability of the auto, the self, to be completely a self, to be completely self-identical. This drive-and-pulse is very much a rhythmic compulsion, or a repetition compulsion, that compulsion to repeat, as we saw in Lacan's Seminar, brought about by the fact that in our imaginary world we are always already symbolic. In the imaginary nothing repeats, no two leaves in the garden are alike, and yet the promise of the trace, in its irreducible binding, is that something will repeat, a promise that inscribes a circularity that is itself already phantasmatic, impossible. By analyzing that desire, deconstruction also reiterates that circle; that is its double bind.

It is when he reflects on this double bind, it seems to me, that Derrida is at his best, that he deflects the sorts of criticisms I aimed at his discourse in previous chapters, criticisms focused on the apparent refusal of duplicity in his writing when he attacks Lacan as a postman of truth, an implicit occupation of the place of truth that Lacan, in his speaking so blatantly of the truth, implicitly refuses to embody. Such a refusal is captured not in the image of a postman fearlessly battling the elements to deliver a letter to its destination, but perhaps more accurately in the image of Ed McMahon's smiling face on a letter addressed to YOU, personally, telling you that YOU may have already won $10,000,000; just return this form to us with a check for X amount to recover your destiny. There is something reminiscent of Nietzsche in this move, actively claiming one's fictions as truths in a motion that simultaneously posits and disavows them as always having been there.[11] It is because Lacan always relies on such necessary duplicity that he can distinguish drive and desire (as if they were really distinguishable): on the one hand, that motion instituted by a "prethetic" and "prejudicative" difference from self with no object and no redemption in sight and, on the other, that belief that the other has what will relieve one's original loss. We can work within the horizons of an ethics of drive, a refusal of the phantasms of desire, but we cannot "renounce its [desire's] laws . . . suspend the order of reason, of meaning, of the question of the origin, of the social bond" (*R* 36). It is precisely because the two ultimately cannot be separated—and here it should become clear that we are also speaking of primary and secondary interpretation—that the discourse of the philosopher, of the one who seeks to tell the truth, must always be duplicitous, must always aim for the production of a speech that is full only insofar as its effect "is to reorder past contingencies by conferring on them the sense of necessities to come" (*R* 58)—a production, that is, of destinies, of teleologies whose truth only holds to the extent that elsewhere we recognize their fiction. It is in this sense that everything I have written here is the truth, a necessary rung in an inexorable ladder of narrative leading up to this conclusion; a reordering of what were before but are no longer mere contingencies has become, in the end, which is also a beginning, the raw materials, the combustible elements of something else, a moment in an interminable chain of interpretation.

Notes

PROLOGUE

1. This statement seems too obvious to footnote, but a brief history running from Susan Sontag's "Against Interpretation," in *Against Interpretation and Other Essays* (New York: Picador, 2001 [1966]) through Michel Foucault's *Archeology of Knowledge*, trans. Sheridan Smith (New York: Pantheon, 1972) to Hans Ulrich Gumbrecht's *Production of Presence: What Meaning Cannot Convey* (Stanford: Stanford University Press, 2004) would at least touch on some milestones. If literary studies is largely divided between historicist tendencies, which hold the dominant position, and theoretical—that is, loosely deconstructive—ones, both can be seen as resisting the urge to say what a texts means.

2. Gianni Vattimo and Aldo Rovatti, *Pensiero Debole* (Milan: Feltrinelli, 1983). It should be noted that if hermeneutics is passé for literary studies, this is not at all the case for philosophy, at least that of the continental variety. See Santiago Zabala's excellent article "Deconstruction, Semantics, and Interpretation," *Aquinas* 48.3 (2005): 669–690. See also *Weakening Philosophy: Essays in Honor of Gianni Vattimo*, ed. Santiago Zabala (Montreal: McGill-Queen's University Press, 2006), and Zabala, *Tugendhat: The Hermeneutical Nature of Analytic Philosophy*, trans. M. Haskell and S. Zabala (New York: Columbia University Press, forthcoming, 2006).

3. Jacques Derrida, *Resistances of Psychoanalysis*, trans. Peggy Kamuf et al. (Stanford: Stanford University Press, 1998), 51.

CHAPTER 1

1. Gilles Deleuze and Félix Guattari, *What Is Philosophy?* trans. Hugh Tomlinson and Graham Burchell (New York: Columbia University Press, 1994), 5.

2. Martin Heidegger, *Unterwegs zur Sprache* (Pfullingen: Naske, 1990), 200, my translation.

3. Jorge Luis Borges, *Obras completas* (Buenos Aires: Emecé, 1974), 772, my translation.

4. This is almost too general a truth to merit citation, but we can certainly refer to one of Derrida's first great books, *Speech and Phenomena*, which is dedicated

to demonstrating that the effort to reduce all indication in order to secure a pure level of expression, and hence universal or essential phenomenological knowledge, is impossible. Jacques Derrida, *Speech and Phenomena*, trans. David B. Allison (Evanston: Northwestern University Press, 1973).

5. See, for example, the contributions by M. H. Abrams and J. Hillis Miller to *Modern Criticism and Theory*, 2nd ed., ed. David Lodge with Nigel Wood (New York: Longman, 2000), 241–330.

6. See Shoshana Felman's discussion of Lacan's insistence on the distinction between meaning and truth, which is also founded on his thinking about truth and reality, which I discuss in the section below. Shoshana Felman, *Writing and Madness* (Stanford: Stanford University Press, 2003), 119–22.

7. Thanks to David E. Johnson for suggesting the *Hamlet* reference.

8. Jean-Luc Nancy, *The Sense of the World*, trans. Jeffrey S. Librett (Minneapolis: University of Minnesota Press, 1993), 35.

9. G. W. F. Hegel, *The Phenomenology of the Spirit*, trans. A. V. Miller (Oxford: Clarendon Press, 1977), 61.

10. As Eco puts it, "It is through the process of interpretation that we cognitively construct worlds, actual and possible." Umberto Eco, *I limiti dell'interpretazione* (Milan: Bompiani, 1990), 12, my translation.

11. The translation of *das Unbewusste* as the unconscious elides, somewhat, the sense of the German, which retains more of its adjectival feel, as in "that which is unconscious." This is clear from the opening paragraph of Freud's essay "Das Unbewusste," where he writes, "We say then, that [these representations] find themselves in the state of the 'Unconscious' "; Sigmund Freud, *Das Ich und das Es: Metapsychologische Schriften* (Frankfurt am Main: Fischer Verlag, 2005), 119, my translation.

12. Martin Heidegger, *Being and Time*, trans. Joan Stambaugh (Albany: State University of New York Press, 1996), 6 (hereafter cited as *BT*).

13. The question may arise if I am merely advocating the practice of productive misreading that Rorty, for example, calls the work of the strong pragmatist. See Richard Rorty, *The Consequences of Pragmatism* (Minneapolis: University of Minnesota Press, 1982), 151. Eco criticizes the notion of the strong misreader as being somewhat less than pragmatist, as he "uses the text to find something outside of the text, something more 'real' than the text itself, that is, the mechanisms of the signifying chain" (Eco 31). I disagree that the reader Rorty is describing finds something more real outside the text. It seems to me that he or she finds something just as real, though—the unconscious—and I am not sure what is unpragmatist about such reading.

14. This statement does not exceed the general horizon of hermeneutics as outlined by Gadamer in *Truth and Method*: "Thus there is no understanding or interpretation in which the totality of this existential structure does not function, even if the intention of the knower is simply to read 'what is there' and to discover

from his sources 'how it really was.' " Hans Georg-Gadamer, *Truth and Method*, 2nd ed., trans. Joel Weinsheimer and Donald G. Marshall (New York: Continuum, 1998), 262. That said, the focus on Heidegger here distances me from Gadamer's hermeneutics, because the former, in the words of Gianni Vattimo, insists on the operativity in the work of art of "a moment of dissolution of historicity, that announces itself as a suspension of hermeneutic continuity of the subject with himself and with his history. The punctuality of the aesthetic consciousness is the way in which the subject lives the leap into the *Ab-grund* [abyss] of his own mortality." Gianni Vattimo, *La fine della modernità* (Milan: Grazanti, 1991), 133, my translation.

15. *BT* 172; Søren Kierkegaard, *The Concept of Anxiety*, trans. Reidar Thomte and Albert B. Anderson (Princeton: Princeton University Press, 1980).

16. Gilles Deleuze and Félix Guattari, *Anti-Oedipus* (Minneapolis: University of Minnesota Press, 1977), 51 (hereafter cited as *AO*).

17. Søren Kierkegaard, *Fear and Trembling/Repetition: Kierkegaard's Writings*, *VI*, trans. Howard V. Hong and Edna H. Hong (Princeton: Princeton University Press, 1983) (hereafter cited as *FT*). These pages follow closely my argument in chapter 3 of *Perversity and Ethics* (Stanford: Stanford University Press, 2005) (hereafter cited as *PE*).

18. To cite one example, see G. William Domhoff, *The Scientific Study of Dreams: Neural Networks, Cognitive Development, and Content Analysis* (Washington, D.C.: American Psychological Association, 2003), 136.

19. Freud was aware of this objection, which he discusses in his *Vorlesungen zur Einfürung in die Psychoanalyse* (Frankfurt am Main: Fischer Verlag, 1999), 203–4.

20. Sigmund Freud, *The Interpretation of Dreams*, trans. James Strachey (New York: Avon Books, 1965), 57 (hereafter cited as *ID*).

21. Immanuel Kant, *The Critique of Pure Reason*, trans. J. M. D. Meiklejohn (Buffalo: Prometheus Books, 1990), 22.

22. René Descartes, *Meditations on First Philosophy*, trans. Donald A. Cress (Indianapolis: Hackett, 1993), 14.

23. Pedro Calderón de la Barca, *Life Is a Dream*, trans. John Clifford (London: N. Hern Books, 1998).

24. Jacques Lacan, *Écrits: A Selection*, trans. Alan Sheridan (New York: Norton, 1977), 170 (hereafter cited as *E*).

25. Michel Foucault, *The History of Sexuality, Volume 1: An Introduction*, trans. Robert Hurley (New York: Vintage Books, 1990), 10.

26. See *PE*, chapter 1.

27. See Jean-Luc Nancy and Philippe Lacoue-Labarthe, *The Title of the Letter*, trans. Francois Raffoul and David Pettigrew (Albany: State University of New York Press, 1992).

28. Barbara Johnson, "The Frame of Reference: Poe, Lacan, Derrida," in *The Purloined Poe: Lacan, Derrida, and Psychoanalytic Reading*, ed. John P. Muller and William J. Richardson (Baltimore: Johns Hopkins University Press, 1988), 213–51.

29. See Lisa Block de Behar, *Borges: The Passion of an Endless Quotation*, trans. William Egginton (Albany: State University of New York Press, 2003), 113.

30. Gilles Deleuze and Félix Guattari, *A Thousand Plateaus*, trans. Brian Massumi (Minneapolis: University of Minnesota Press, 1987), 154.

31. See my discussion in *PE,* chapter 1.

32. Jacques-Alain Miller, "Extimacy," in *Lacanian Theory of Discourse*, ed. Mark Bracher, Marshall W. Alcorn, Jr., Ronald J. Corthell, and Françoise Massardier-Kennedy (New York: New York University Press, 1994), 74–87.

33. Jacques Lacan, *The Seminar of Jacques Lacan, Book VII: The Ethics of Psychoanalysis 1959–1960*, trans. Dennis Porter (New York: W. W. Norton & Co., 1992), 2.

34. Jean Laplanche and J.-B. Pontalis, "Fantasy and the Origins of Sexuality," *The International Journal of Psychoanalysis* 49.1 (1968): 1–18.

35. *ID* 547–48 and Jacques Lacan, *The Four Fundamental Concepts of Psycho-Analysis*, trans. Alan Sheridan (New York: W. W. Norton & Co., 1977), 59.

36. Freud, *Vorlesungen*, 206.

CHAPTER 2

1. Daniel Paul Schreber, *Denkwürdigkeiten eines Nervenkranken* (Leipzig: Oswald Mutze, 1903), translated as *Memoirs of My Nervous Illness*, trans. Ida Macalpine and Richard A. Hunter (London: W. Dawson, 1955). See also Eric Santner's *My Own Private Germany: Daniel Paul Schreber's Secret History of Modernity* (Princeton: Princeton University Press, 1996).

2. Sigmund Freud, *Studienausgabe*, Band VII (Frankfurt: Fischer, 1994), 135. The original case study, cited below in translation, is to be found on 133–203 of that volume.

3. "We must be referred to an order, then, that resists philosophy's founding opposition between the sensible and the intelligible." Later, in the same text, "These oppositions do not pertain in the least to differance, and this, no doubt, is what makes thinking about it difficult and uncomfortable." Jacques Derrida, "Differance," in *Speech and Phenomena*, trans. David B. Allison (Evanston: Northwestern University Press, 1973), 133, 142 (hereafter cited as *D*).

4. Immanuel Kant, *The Critique of Pure Reason*, trans. Norman Kemp Smith (New York: Modern Library, 1958), 5.

5. René Descartes, *Discourse on the Method*, trans. George Heffernon (South Bend, Ind.: University of Notre Dame Press, 1994).

6. G. W. F. Hegel, *The Phenomenology of the Spirit*, trans. A. V. Miller (Oxford: Clarendon Press, 1977), 66.

7. Jacques Derrida, *Aporias*, trans. Thomas Dutroit (Stanford: Stanford University Press, 1993), 79. Thanks are owed to Isabella Winkler for drawing my attention to this and many of the other Derridean points presented here.

8. Derrida makes this argument most forcefully in "Khora," in *On the Name*, trans. David Wood, John P. Leavey, and Ian Mcleod (Stanford: Stanford University Press, 1995). See Tina Chanter's excellent discussion in her "Abjection, Death and Difficult Reasoning: The Impossibility of Naming Chora in Kristeva and Derrida," *Tympanum* 4 (2000): http://www.usc.edu/dept/complit/tympanum/4/.

9. Isabella Winkler writes about this in her dissertation, "Quodlibet: The affirmation of the singular in recent continental thought from Derrida to Deleuze," dissertation, University at Buffalo, 2003.

10. Jacques Derrida, *Points . . . : Interviews, 1974–1994*, ed. Elisabeth Weber, trans. Peggy Kamuf et al. (Stanford: Stanford University Press, 1995), 119, qtd. in Winkler.

11. Sigmund Freud, *Three Case Histories* (New York: Simon & Schuster, 1963), 99 (hereafter cited as *TCH*).

12. See the above references to "Differance."

13. The allusion is to Santner's book.

14. See Pierre-Gilles Gueguen's helpful discussion in "Transference as Deception," in *Reading Seminar XI: Lacan's Four Fundamental Concepts of Psychoanalysis*, ed. Richard Feldstein, Bruce Fink, and Maire Janus (Albany: State University of New York Press, 1995), 77–90.

15. See *PE,* chapter 1.

16. Jacques Lacan, *The Seminar of Jacques Lacan: Book III: The Psychoses*, ed. Jacques-Alain Miller, trans. Russell Grigg (New York: W. W. Norton & Company, 1993), 321 (hereafter cited as *III*).

17. Again, *PE,* chapter 1.

18. G. W. F. Hegel, *Ästhetik,* 2 vols. (Stuttgart: Reclam, 1976), 119.

19. See my *How the World Became a Stage: Presence, Theatricality, and the Question of Modernity* (Albany: State University of New York Press, 2003).

20. See section 56 of the *Monadology.* G. W. Leibniz's *Monadology: An Edition for Students*, ed. Nicholas Rescher (Pittsburgh: University of Pittsburgh Press, 1991), 198. The reference to Deleuze is to his *The Fold: Leibniz and the Baroque*, trans. Tom Conley (Minneapolis: University of Minnesota Press, 1993).

21. Tim Dean, for example, has argued forcefully against the usefulness of the term in his *Beyond Sexuality* (Chicago: University of Chicago Press, 2000).

22. Juliet Mitchell, *Psychoanalysis and Feminism: Freud, Reich, Laing and Women* (New York: Vintage Books, 1975), 364.

23. The mention of the thing, *das Ding*, is intentional here, for if the psychotic mechanism depends on a return *in* the real of something that has been refused in

this utter and abject way from the symbolic, then Lacan's thinking also demonstrates that all subjects organize their psychical reality around such fundamental exclusion, which is the real itself. What is crucial to recognize is that in the case of the psychotic mechanism what is refused or excluded is this very primordial exclusion itself, in that no signifier ever arises to stand in for it.

24. *The Standard Edition of the Complete Psychological Works* of *Sigmund Freud*, 24 vols., ed. J. Strachey (London: Hogarth Press, 1953–1974), 11: 155–61.

25. It should be clear that this division is itself an interpretation of Kant's tripartite scheme of the thing, the phenomenon, and the understanding, in that order. See below.

26. Immanuel Kant, *Critique of Pure Reason*, trans. Paul Guyer and Allen W. Wood (New York: Cambridge University Press, 1998), 257.

27. See the discussion below of Roa Bastos's novel, "I the Supreme" (*Yo el supremo*), whose paranoid dictator dictates in a style that desperately produces ever more neologisms. Augusto Roa Bastos, *Yo el supremo* (Madrid: Cátedra, 1987).

28. See "Aggressivity in Psychoanalysis" in Jacques Lacan, *Écrits: A Selection*, trans. Alan Sheridan (New York: Norton, 1977), 8–29.

29. The classic analytic critique of this representationalist model is to be found in Donald Davidson's essay "On the Very Idea of a Conceptual Scheme," *Proceedings and Addresses of the American Philosophical Association* 47 (1974).

30. The term comes from Tim Dean, who has used it in lectures as well as in his teaching.

31. Of course Heidegger did not really say it like that: "To bring to language ever and again this advent of being that remains, and in its remaining waits for human beings, is the sole matter of thinking. For this reason essential thinkers always say the Same. But that does not mean the identical. Of course they say it only to one who undertakes to meditate on them." Martin Heidegger, "Letter on Humanism," trans. Frank A. Capuzzi, in *Pathmarks*, ed. William McNeill (Cambridge: Cambridge University Press, 1998), 275. This is, in my reading, the reason why Heidegger does not often engage in polemics but prefers reading "essential thinkers" as saying the same thing he is saying, albeit differently.

32. See, for example, Brian Greene, *The Fabric of the Cosmos: Space, Time, and the Texture of Reality* (New York: Knopf, 2005), 79.

33. These examples are surely reminiscent of many others from similar discussions in the philosophy of language, particularly those regarding the problem of naming. Perhaps the most influential theory in this domain is that of Saul Kripke, who chose the term *rigid designator* for those terms that designate the same object in every possible world. For Kripke, names are examples of rigid designators, which means that we will tend to use them irrespective of changes in circumstantial knowledge. In the example I stipulated, we will continue to use the name Shakespeare regardless of changing knowledge about the identity of the man and whether

he in fact wrote his plays or not. On the other hand, if we find out that "Shakespeare" did not exist, in the sense that his "real name" was not that but something else, we may in fact continue to call him Shakespeare regardless. In *The Sublime Object of Ideology*, Žižek identifies the rigid designator, which remains the same over the course of a series of changing attributes, with the Lacanian master signifier, or quilting point. The quilting point has the function of quilting a field of meaning together while failing to mean itself. Names, master signifiers, and quilting points, in other words, all function as points of certainty in what follows. See Saul Kripke, *Naming and Necessity* (Cambridge: Harvard University Press, 1980), excerpted in *The Philosophy of Language*, 2nd ed., ed. A. P. Martinich (New York: Oxford University Press, 1990), 281; and Slavoj Žižek, *The Sublime Object of Ideology* (London: Verso, 1989).

34. See David E. Johnson, "Kant's Dog," *Diacritics* 34.1 (2004): 19–39.

35. Sigmund Freud, *Neue Folge der Vorlesungen zur Einführung in die Psychoanalyse* (Wien: Internationaler Psychoanalytischer Verlag, 1933), 31.

36. In *Perversity and Ethics*, passim.

37. *Spur* is also German for mark or trace.

38. See William Egginton, "Psychoanalysis and the *Comedia:* Skepticism and the Paternal Function in *La vida es sueño*," *Bulletin of the Comediantes* 52.1 (2000): 97–122.

39. Slavoj Žižek has emphasized a less "generous" reading, at least of Deleuze and Guattari's work together, asking, "[W]hat inherent impasse caused Deleuze to turn toward Guattari? Is Anti-Oedipus, arguably Deleuze's worst book, not the result of escaping the full confrontation of a deadlock via a simplified 'flat' solution . . . ?" Slavoj Žižek, *Organs Without a Body: On Deleuze and Consequences* (London: Routledge, 2004), 20–21. While this may be the case, I would argue that it still makes sense, if writing from a psychoanalytic perspective, to confront the anti-psychoanalytic thesis of a thinker head on rather than dismiss it. In that light, I will focus on Deleuze's work with Guattari in these pages.

40. Gilles Deleuze and Félix Guattari, *A Thousand Plateaus*, trans. Brian Massumi (Minneapolis: University of Minnesota Press, 1987), 117 (hereafter cited as *TP*). See also Claire Colebrook, "Postmodernism Is a Humanism: Deleuze and Equivocity," *Women: A Cultural Review* 15.3 (2004): 283–307.

41. Gilles Deleuze and Félix Guattari, *What Is Philosophy?*, trans. Hugh Tomlinson and Graham Burchell (New York: Columbia University Press), 40 (hereafter cited as *WP*). Qtd. in Gregg Lambert, *The Non-Philosophy of Gilles Deleuze* (London: Continuum, 2002), 6.

42. Claire Colebrook, *Gilles Deleuze* (New York: Routledge, 2002), 72–79.

43. Gilles Deleuze and Félix Guattari, *Anti-Oedipus: Capitalism and Schizophrenia* (Minneapolis: University of Minnesota Press, 1983), 24 (hereafter cited as *AO*).

44. Cited in Thomas Sheehan, "A Paradigm Shift in Heidegger Research," *Continental Philosophy Review* 32, 2 (2001): 1–20, 11. Sheehan also argues that we

should cease leaving Dasein untranslated, as I have done here—because, although I understand and largely agree with the reasoning behind it, this is not strictly an inquiry into Heidegger's thought, and therefore the specifics of the equivalences between *Da, Welt,* and *Lichtung* are not overly important here.

45. Daniel C. Dennett, *Consciousness Explained* (New York: Little, Brown and Company, 1991). The best discussion of classical realism and some contemporary alternatives is Hilary Putnam's *Realism with a Human Face* (Cambridge: Harvard University Press, 1990). See esp. 3–42. For an example of "radical realism," see Edward Pols, *Radical Realism: Direct Knowing in Science and Philosophy* (Ithaca: Cornell University Press, 1992), esp. 24.

46. Jorge Luis Borges, *Obras completas*, vol. 1 (Buenos Aires: Emecé, 1996), 489, my translation.

47. This is because any perspective, by definition, is located in space and time. As Brian Greene writes, even if absolute spacetime exists and provides a final reference point for motion, nevertheless "observers in relative motion do not agree on simultaneity—they do not agree on what things happen at the same time" (57). If simultaneity is observer dependent, then it is clear that there can be no sense to the idea of an "objective," i.e., observer-independent, location in spacetime to all the socks I have lost over my life, as that would also require that all observers agree on the median time of their loss, which they cannot do.

48. Gilles Deleuze, *Bergsonism*, trans. Hugh Tomlinson and Barbara Habberjam (New York: Zone, 1991), 17 (hereafter cited as *B*). See also Elizabeth Grosz's discussion in *The Nick of Time: Politics, Evolution, and the Untimely* (Durham: Duke University Press, 2005), 155–84.

49. Gilles Deleuze, *Differences and Repetition*, trans. Paul Patton (New York: Columbia University Press, 1994), qtd. in Lambert 16.

50. We should remark in passing that as arcane as this discussion may appear, it is in fact germane to cosmological discussions of the day. For example, the *New York Times* featured an article in the Science Times section (10/29/02) concerning the debate in contemporary physics around the possibility of multiple universes.

51. Briane Greene catalogues this theory among other possible but probably nonconfirmable descriptions of cosmic reality (Greene 205–8).

52. This is also the problem with the position now being defended by the so-called intelligent design movement, whose proponents fault the theory of evolution for denying prima facie a solution to the apparently astronomical odds against something as extraordinarily complex as life having emerged without guidance of some kind. What this argument fails to note is that our very position as admirers of this complexity is itself a result of that complexity and hence of those odds. If you have just won the lottery, it may feel like God had a hand in selecting you, but the several million who did not select the winning ticket might see it differently.

53. Qtd. in Dennis Overbye, "A New View of Our Universe: One of Many," *The New York Times*, October 29, 2002, national edition, D1.

54. Gilles Deleuze, *The Fold: Leibniz and the Baroque*, trans. Tom Conley (Minneapolis: University of Minnesota Press, 1993), 82; qtd. and discussed in Lambert 29.

55. Gilles Deleuze, *Negotiations: 1972–1990*, trans. Martin Joughin (New York: Columbia University Press, 1995), 6.

CHAPTER 3

1. Jacques Lacan, *Écrits* (Paris: Seuil, 1966), 10, my translation. The main ideas in his treatment of "The Purloined Letter" are first announced in his seminar of 1954–1955, published in English as *The Seminar of Jacques Lacan: Book II: The Ego in Freud's Theory and in the Technique of Psychoanalysis, 1954–1955*, trans. Sylvana Tomaselli (New York: Norton, 1991).

2. Gilles Deleuze, *Differences and Repetition*, trans. Paul Patton (New York: Columbia University Press, 1994), 17.

3. Jacques Derrida, *The Post Card: From Socrates to Freud and Beyond*, trans. Alan Bass (Chicago: University of Chicago Press, 1987), qtd. in Martin Hägglund, "The Necessity of Discrimination: Disjoining Derrida and Levinas," *Diacritics* 34.1 (2004): 40–71.

4. The term comes from friend Joshua Landy, who uses it as an epithet for people like me.

5. Martin Heidegger, *Being and Time*, trans. Joan Stambaugh (Albany: State University of New York Press, 1996), 50 (hereafter cited as *BT*).

6. Thanks to Andrea Spain for bringing this argument to my attention.

7. An excellent example of this argument is to be found in Heidegger's reworking of the traditional definition of truth as *adaequatio intellectus et rei* (*BT* 198–201). The sentence that encapsulates my argument above is this one: "Being-true as discovering is in turn ontologically possible only on the basis of being-in-the-world" (201). See Christopher Fynsk's discussion in his *Heidegger, Thought, and Historicity* (Ithaca: Cornell University Press, 1986), 86–87.

8. Jacques Lacan, "Seminar on the 'Purloined Letter,'" trans. Jeffrey Mehlman, *The Purloined Poe: Lacan, Derrida, and Psychoanalytic Reading*, ed. John P. Muller and William J. Richardson (Baltimore: Johns Hopkins University Press, 1988), 35 (hereafter cited as *PL*).

9. Lacan illustrates this operation with the now-famous joke in which one man accuses the other of deceiving him about his ultimate destination by deliberately telling him the truth, all the while knowing that the truth will be taken as a lie.

10. Lacan elaborates on this time in his article, "Le temps logique et l'assertion de certitude anticipeé," in *Écrits* (Paris: Seuil, 1966), 197–214.

11. As Lacan puts it in the earlier seminar: "for the policemen the truth doesn't matter, for them there is only reality, and that is why they don't find anything." Lacan, II 202.

12. Jorge Luis Borges, *Obras completas*, vol. III (Buenos Aires: Emecé, 1996), 51.

13. Jacques Derrida, "The Purveyor of Truth," trans. Alan Bass, *The Purloined Poe: Lacan, Derrida, and Psychoanalytic Reading*, ed. John P. Muller and William J. Richardson (Baltimore: Johns Hopkins University Press, 1988), 174 (hereafter cited as *PT*).

14. See Luiz Costa Lima, "Social Representation and Mimesis," *New Literary History* 16.3 (1985): 447–66, esp. p. 454.

15. Jacques Lacan, *Écrits: A Selection*, trans. Alan Sheridan (New York: W. W. Norton, 1977), 51.

16. Lacan, *Écrits: A Selection,* 146–78.

17. Derrida's critique of the ideality of the signified finds its origin in his first major book, a deconstruction of the notions of expression and indication in Husserl's phenomenology. The problem is that what is indeed a brilliant critique of the ideality of the signified in Husserl is transposed onto Lacan's theory as if Lacan were saying the same thing; in fact, however, Lacan's position here is much closer to Derrida's than to Husserl's. In *Speech and Phenomena* Derrida attributes this notion of ideality to Husserl: "Insofar as the unity of the word—what lets it be recognized as a word, the *same* word, the unity of a sound pattern and a sense—is not to be confused with the multiple sensible events of its employment or taken to depend on them, the *sameness* of the word is ideal; it is the ideal possibility of repetition, and it loses nothing by the reduction of *any* empirical event marked by its appearance, nor all of them." Jacques Derrida, *Speech and Phenomena*, trans. David B. Allison (Evanston: Northwestern University Press, 1973), 41 (hereafter cited as *SP*). So far, so good. But what Derrida objects to and in fact demolishes in his analysis is the notion that indicative speech is in a relation of representation to the ideality of expressive speech and that ideality therefore underlies the possibility of repetition. In contrast, as he argues, "By reason of the primordially repetitive structure of signs in general, there is every likelihood that 'effective' language is just as imaginary as imaginary speech, and that imaginary speech is just as effective as effective speech. In both expression and indicative communication the difference between reality and representation, between the veridical and the imaginary, and between simple presence and repetition has begun to wear away" (51). In other words, it is the repetitive structure that undergirds our perception of ideality, and not the reverse. But this is exactly what Lacan is saying in the seminar. So Derrida is not arguing against Lacan here, but rather resuscitating an older argument with classical phenomenology, which he misreads Lacan as importing into his discourse.

18. Jacques Derrida, *Resistances of Psychoanalysis*, trans. Peggy Kamuf et al. (Stanford: Stanford University Press, 1998), 51 (hereafter cited as *RP*).

19. Just in case this is still not clear: the word *apple* indicating the apple in front of us, not admitting of partition—that is, being the same in the face of the infinite differences of imaginary apples and their spatial and temporal aspects—cannot achieve self-identity because its purpose, its essence, is to always indicate something other than itself.

20. See Jacques Lacan, *Le séminaire, livre XVII, L'enverse de la psychanalyse* (Paris: Seuil, 1991), 103: "However, this position is strictly untenable; it constitutes an infraction of the rule as regards the function of the signifier, which can signify anything except, surely, itself." My translation.

21. As Derrida insists, "The *Bedeutung* [meaning] 'I am' or 'I am alive' or 'my living present is' is what it is, has the real identity proper to all *Bedeutung*, only if it is not impaired by falsity, that is, if I can be dead at the moment it is functioning . . . its possibility requires the possibility that I be dead" (*SP* 96–97). This is exactly right, and not at all what I mean by speaking from a position that is only possible if one were already dead, which is what Lacan accuses Derrida of.

22. See Slavoj Žižek, *For They Know Not What They Do: Enjoyment as a Political Factor* (London: Verso, 1991), 170–71. Here Žižek brings all these elements together seamlessly in a joke he recounts about a conscript who gets out of military service by feigning to be mad. He ceaselessly repeats the desperate line "That's not it!" until a psychiatrist, finally convinced he is mad, gives him the document releasing him from service, at which point "he says cheerfully: 'That's it!'" Žižek uses the joke to illustrate how "the ill-famed Hegelian 'teleology of Reason' has to be grasped: the End towards which the movement tends is not given in advance, it is so to speak created by the movement itself—the necessary deception consists in the fact that for this movement to take place, the subjects must overlook how their own search created what they 'find' at the end." The joke, then, as he points out, is ultimately about "*how a letter always arrives at its destination.*"

23. See my *Perversity and Ethics* (Stanford: Stanford University Press, 2005), chapter 3.

24. See Barbara Herrnstein-Smith, *Contingencies of Values: Alternative Perspectives for Critical Theory* (Cambridge, Mass.: Harvard University Press, 1988), 113.

CHAPTER 4

1. We can begin by quoting Borges, himself referring to Bergson: "time is an essential problem. I mean that we cannot do without time. Our consciousness is continuously passing from one state to another, and that is time: succession. I believe Henri Bergson said that time was the capital problem of metaphysics. If that problem had been resolved, all would have been resolved. Happily, I don't think there is any danger that it will be resolved." Jorge Luis Borges, *Obras completas,* vol. IV (Buenos Aires: Emecé, 1996), 199, my translation.

2. My thanks to David E. Johnson for pointing me to this wonderful anecdote, which can be found in James Irby, Napoleón Murat, and Carlos Peralta, *Encuentro con Borges* (Buenos Aires: Editorial Galerna, 1968), 108, my translation.

3. Gabriel García Márquez, *Cien años de soledad* (Madrid: Espasa Calpe, 1983), 93, my translation.

4. Xavier Zubiri, *Sobre la esencia* (Madrid: Alianza Editorial, 1985), 455–517.

5. Martin Heidegger, *Sein und Zeit* (Tübingen: Max Niemeyer Verlag, 1986), 83–89. English translation by Joan Stambaugh, *Being and Time* (Albany: State University of New York Press, 1996), 77–83 (hereafter cited as *SZ* and *BT,* respectively).

6. Jorge Luis Borges, *Obras completas*, vol. II (Buenos Aires, Emecé, 1996), 148–49, my translation.

7. *Eigentlich.* See discussion in the following sections.

8. "Since the trace is the intimate relation of the living present with its outside, the openness upon exteriority in general, upon the sphere of what is not 'one's own,' etc., the temporalization of sense is, from the outset, a 'spacing.' As soon as we admit spacing both as 'interval' or difference and as openness upon the outside, there can no longer be any absolute inside, for the 'outside' has insinuated itself into the movement by which the inside of the nonspatial, which is called 'time,' appears, is constitutes, is 'presented.'" Jacques Derrida, *Speech and Phenomena*, trans. David B. Allison (Evanston: Northwestern University Press, 1973), 86.

9. Or "an open field of sense-making relations," in Sheehan's words. See Thomas Sheehan, "A Paradigm Shift in Heidegger Research," *Continental Philosophy Review* 32, 2 (2001): 1–20, esp. p. 11.

10. Jorge Luis Borges, *Obras completas*, vol. I (Buenos Aires: Emecé, 1996), 486, my translation.

11. See the discussion of Heidegger and Derrida below.

12. Jacques Derrida, *Margins of Philosophy*, trans. Alan Bass (Chicago: University of Chicago Press, 1982), 326.

13. Augusto Roa Bastos, *Yo el supremo* (Madrid: Cátedra, 1987), 102, my translation.

14. See Jacques Derrida, "La pharmacie de Plato," in *La dissemination* (Paris: Seuil, 1979), 120.

15. Jacques Derrida, *Margins of Philosophy*, trans. Alan Bass. (Chicago: University of Chicago Press, 1982), 61 (hereafter cited as *MP*).

16. From here on references to *Being and Time* will be to Heidegger's original (*SZ*). In all cases I have consulted Joan Stambaugh's translation and Magda King's commentary and have altered their translations where necessary. Magda King, *A Guide to Heidegger's* Being and Time, ed. John Llewelyn (Albany: State University of New York Press, 2001).

17. Derrida is here using the Latin transcription of the Greek νυν, *nun*, which also means "now" in German.

18. Borges also states the aporia in a characteristically concise way: "What is the present moment? The present moment is the moment that entails a little of the past and a little of the future. The present in itself is like the finite point of geometry. The present in itself does not exist" (Borges, IV 202).

19. See *SZ* 421.

20. See Tina Chanter's insightful discussion of this debate in her *Time, Death, and the Feminine: Levinas with Heidegger* (Stanford: Stanford University Press, 2001).

21. By spatial world I mean more or less what Heidegger calls being-in-the-world (*in-der-Welt-sein*). Rather than a being finding itself in a world, like water can be found in a glass, *Dasein* is its being-in-the-world.

22. For a pragmatist reading of the role of temporality in Heidegger, see Mike Sandbothe, *The Temporalization of Time*, trans. Andrew Lipkin (New York: Rowman & Littlefield, 2001), 83–109.

23. Although this is enough for our purposes, the argument actually goes a little further and is best exposed by Kant in his argument with Mendelssohn on the subject of the persistence of the soul. If there is a simple substance (soul), so Mendelssohn's argument goes, a change in that substance from one minimal unit of time to the next must take place for any change in it to take place. Either the substance can change from one unit to the next gradually (through disintegration), but if it is a simple substance that is impossible; or it can change drastically, but this would entail its vanishing and replacement by something new and hence not a persisting at all. Mendelssohn argues that the latter is impossible because it assumes a change from something to nothing can take place over an interval $t = 0$, which would mean the something would have to be simultaneously something and nothing, a contradiction. He thus adduces the impossibility of either option as proof of the persistence of an unchanging (i.e., eternal) soul. Kant's response is to insist that although extensive magnitude requires time in order to diminish to zero a truly simple substance could certainly be imagined that would have an *intensive* magnitude, which could vary down to zero regardless of the restrictions of space and time. Therefore, Kant argues, Mendelssohn's argument for the persistence of the soul fails, and in fact no such proof can work. Immanuel Kant, *Critique of Pure Reason*, trans. Paul Guyer and Allen W. Wood (Cambridge: Cambridge University Press, 1998), 449. See also Thomas Powell's discussion in "Kant, Elanguescence, and Degrees of Reality," *Philosophy and Phenomenological Research* 46.2 (1985): 199–217.

24. Datability (*Datierbarkeit*) designates the way in which Dasein, in its everydayness, refers to events and things with notes like "now," "then," and "on that former occasion" (*SZ* 408).

25. In a formulation that sounds similarly paradoxical, Derrida speaks of "essential corruptibility," of a being for whom corruptibility—that which traditionally is defined as not pertaining to essence—is its essence. See Hägglund's

discussion in Martin Hägglund, "The Necessity of Discrimination: Disjoining Derrida and Levinas," *Diacritics* 34.1 (2004): 40–71.

26. Henri Bergson, *Creative Evolution*, trans. Arthur Mitchell (New York: Henry Holt and Company, 1911), 2. Duration is a "becoming that endures," in Deleuze's words, contributing "an internal succession that is both heterogeneous and continuous." Gilles Deleuze, *Bergsonism*, trans. Hugh Tomlinson and Barbara Habberjam (New York: Zone Books, 1991), 37. These formulations seem to me to be compatible with ecstatic unity.

27. Heidegger himself had a somewhat different, underdeveloped, objection to Bergson: his notion of "externalized" or "spatialized" time fails to take into account that what Heidegger is calling "vulgar" time is nevertheless a "genuine phenomenon of time" (*SZ* 333) and, while derivative of original time, cannot be dismissed as a mere spatialization. While King is certainly correct in her judgment that Bergson's notions of "qualitative" and "spatialized" time correspond in some degree to Heidegger's distinction between "original" and "vulgar" time and that Heidegger's criticism is thus "of an uncalled-for severity" (King 376), when taken in light of his reading in *Kant and the Problem of Metaphysics*, as we will see below, Heidegger's objection certainly seems to hold, namely, that time as the series of nows springs forth from the transcendental power of the imagination—itself inseparable from the spacing of the concept, and hence self-consciousness—and that divisibility into discrete moments cannot therefore be relegated to some belated state of awareness. The notion of duration continues to provoke confusion in contemporary followers of Bergson as well. Even Elizabeth Grosz must write of duration that on the one hand, "Each duration, each movement, each act forms a continuity, a single, indivisible whole," whereas on the other hand "When duration is divided, which fundamentally transforms its nature, it can be regarded as time." Elizabeth Grosz, *The Nick of Time: Politics, Evolution, and the Untimely* (Durham: Duke University Press, 2005), 183.

28. Gilles Deleuze, *Difference and Repetition*, trans. Paul Patton (New York: Columbia University Press, 1994), 81. Thanks to Andrea Spain for bringing these passages to my attention.

29. Elsewhere Deleuze writes, "Since the past is constituted not after the present that it was but at the same time, time has to split itself in two at each moment as present and past, which differ from each other in nature, or, what amounts to the same thing, it has to split the present in two heterogeneous directions, one of which is launched toward the future while the other falls into the past" (Gilles Deleuze, *Time Image* 81, qtd. in D. N. Rodowick, *Gilles Deleuze's Time Machine* [Durham: Duke University Press, 1997], 82). The problem with this formulation is that if the present is something that has to be split, we are back in the realm of the aporia because it is then a thing or a presence that itself negates time.

30. John McCumber's excellent discussion of what he calls the "diakenic" relation between authenticity and inauthenticity is relevant here. As he argues, Heidegger may have intended to write *Being and Time* from an authentic perspective, but if he did, he failed. Rather, neither authenticity nor inauthenticity "is derived from the other, and no higher unity is possible; but both . . . define each other and Dasein itself." John McCumber, *Metaphysics and Oppression: Heidegger's Challenge to Western Philosophy* (Bloomington: Indiana University Press, 1999), 212. The emphasis I am proposing on ecstatic unity seems to me to capture an authenticity that would be in such a relation with inauthenticity.

31. An analogous shift is at work in attempts to describe the "expansion" of the universe: while the universe has expanded to its current dimensions from a point of unimaginable density, it is misleading to think—along with the imagery of the "big bang" model—of a single point expanding ever outward, because the whole idea of the *universe* is that there would have been no space *outside* it in which to expand. The size in question is measured in terms of internal distances, and not against some externally existing standard.

32. As Hägglund deftly demonstrates, the notion of an absolutely other is nothing other than an ultimate vindication for an absolutely same, and hence a rigorously temporal understanding of time would have to be its own alterity: "Indeed, Levinas speaks of the wholly Other instead of the wholly Same. But this makes no essential difference since these two extremes—as Derrida maintains in 'Violence and Metaphysics'—invert into each other and at bottom are founded on the same ideal."

33. Martin Heidegger, *Kant and the Problem of Metaphysics*, trans. Richard Taft, 5th ed. (Bloomington: Indiana University Press, 1997), 123 (hereafter cited as *KPM*).

34. Kant: "The concept of a dog signifies a rule in accordance with which my imagination can specify the shape of a four-footed animal in general, without being restricted to any single particular shape that experience offers me or any possible image that I can exhibit *in concreto*" (273). David E. Johnson makes the connection between Kant's and Funes's dogs, arguing that Kant's dog must be dead and that this diagnosis emerges from Borges's treatment of Funes and his dog: "Why is Kant's dog always already dead? The dog is dead because it can exist only insofar as it is temporal; yet, in order to be conceived it cannot be temporal." As Johnson works out, schematism as the fundamental operation of the imagination provides the temporal determination that allows for something to become an object of experience; however, the spontaneity of the same imagination means that misattribution will remain an unavoidable possibility. "For this reason he ties the imagination to a ground that remains unaffected by time, to a 'pure, original, unchanging consciousness' (Kant 232), the 'standing and lasting I' that 'constitutes the correlate of all our representations' (240): 'transcendental apperception' (232)." David E. Johnson, "Kant's Dog," *Diacritics* 34.1 (2004): 19–39. According to Johnson,

what Funes represents is a temporal synthesis whose spontaneity, whose play, has not been reined in, put on a leash, hence killed, by the immobility of the transcendental apperception.

35. As Derrida writes, "[t]ime is *spacing*. It is the relation of space to itself, its for-itself" (*MP* 43). Heidegger's note that it must also be considered as ecstatically *in-itself* merely specifies that in the for-itself of spacing cannot be considered as the relation to itself of two or more integral moments of space; rather, its auto-alterity is all encompassing; nothing escapes it. See Hägglund's definition of the trace as "constitutive spacing," which I discuss below. Finally, I wrote about spacing and Funes in "Sobre el espaciamiento," which I first delivered as a talk in Lima, Peru, in April 2003, and which was published in Spanish as "Sobre el espaciamiento: El espacio paranoico del Dr. Francia." In *Espacios y discursos compartidos en la literatura de América Latina: Actas del Coloquio Internacional del Comité de Estudios Latinoamericanos de la Asociación Internacional de Literatura Comparada*, ed. Biagio D'Angelo (Lima: Fondo Editorial de la Universidad Católica Sedes Sapientiae-Fondo, Editorial de la Universidad Nacional Mayor de San Marcos, 2003), 102–10.

36. See Johnson's thorough discussion of Locke and Borges in "Kant's Dog."

37. As Sylvia Molloy points out, the very narrating of Funes's perception would be impossible: "The series in 'Funes' and in 'The Aleph' only exist in perception itself; it [*sic*] cannot be told." Sylvia Molloy, *Signs of Borges*, trans. Oscar Montero (Durham: Duke University Press, 1994), 118.

38. This minimum capacity corresponds to what Kant calls the synthesis of reproduction: "But if I were always to lose the preceding representations (the first parts of the line, the preceding parts of time, or the successively represented units) from my thoughts and not reproduce them when I proceed to the following ones, then no whole representation and none of the previously mentioned thoughts, not even the purest and most fundamental representations of space and time, could ever arise" (Kant 230). Heidegger's argument that the ecstasy of temporality is always already a unity can be seen as a positive correlate to Rorty's pithy deflation of this position in Kant: "How, in other words, do we know that a manifold which cannot be represented as a manifold *is* a manifold? More generally, if we are going to argue that we can only be conscious of synthesized intuitions, how do we get our information about intuitions prior to synthesis?" Richard Rorty, *Philosophy and the Mirror of Nature* (Princeton: Princeton University Press, 1979), 154.

39. At first glance, Heidegger's and Borges's point would seem to be a repetition of what Edmund Husserl, Heidegger's teacher, wrote in his *Phenomenology of Internal Time Consciousness*: "We could not speak of a temporal succession of tones if . . . what is earlier would have vanished without a trace and only what is momentarily sensed would be given to our apprehension." Edmund Husserl, *The*

Phenomenology of Internal Time Consciousness, trans. James S. Churchill (Bloomington: Indiana University Press, 1964), qtd. in Francisco Varela, "The Specious Present: A Neurophenomenology of Time Consciousness," in *Naturalizing Phenomenology: Issues in Contemporary Phenomenology and Cognitive Science*, ed. J. Petitot, F. J. Varela, J. M. Roy, and B. Pachoud (Stanford: Stanford University Press, 1999), qtd. online at http://web.ccr.jussieu.fr/varela/human_consciousness/article02.html#I1, page 10. But Husserl's entire emphasis is on the unity of the now in its retention: "For only in primary remembrance do we see what is past; only in it is the past constituted, i.e. not in a representative but in a presentative way. . . . It is the essence of primary remembrance to bring this new and unique moment to primary, direct intuition, just as it is the essence of the perception of the now to bring the now directly to intuition" (qtd. in Varela 10). Varela quotes this approvingly, stating "Nowness, in this perspective, is therefore pre-semantic in that it does not require a rememoration . . . in order to emerge" (Varela 8). Varela and Husserl, therefore, find the present to be a full moment, pre-semantic, immediately present to primary and direct intuition. With Borges, Heidegger, and Derrida, I am arguing precisely the opposite.

40. Borges I, 248, my translation.

41. Juan Nuño, *La filosofía de Borges* (Mexico City: Fondo de Cultura Económica, 1986), 114, my translation. Víctor Bravo, in contrast, regards this fascination with the infinite and the total as an intractable aspect of the paradoxes inherent to the limit. Víctor Bravo, *El orden y la paradoja: Jorge Luis Borges y el pensamiento de la modernidad* (Mérida, Venezuela: Universidad de los Andes, Ediciones del Vicerectorado Académico, 2003), 263–68. See also W. H. Bossart's study of time in his *Borges and Philosophy* (New York: Peter Lang, 2003), 79–108. He too agrees that Borges ultimately reuses the consolations of the eternal: "But avoiding this contradiction is impossible since to write about the unreality of time, one must use language, and our language is saturated with time" (93).

42. In the story Borges describes the emergence of fictional objects into "our" reality as a result of humanity's tendency to be enchanted by "whatever symmetry with an appearance of order" but then specifies that it is not merely the order that is at fault and that contributes to such enchantments as "dialectical materialism, anti-Semitism, and Nazism." Rather, it is the failure to distinguish the order from the source of its ordering. "Enchanted by its rigor, humanity forgets and forgets again that it is a rigor of chess masters, not of angels." In other words, by attributing to a manmade rigor the perfection of the absolute, humanity forgets that it cannot occupy that place, a place from which, as I argued above, constitutive spacing would be obliterated. These passages were quoted from Borges I, 442–43, my translation.

43. Luis Kancyper gets this right, it seems to me, in his psychoanalytic reading of temporality in Borges, *Jorge Luis Borges, o la passion de la amistad: Estudio psicoanalítico* (Buenos Aires: Grupo Editorial Lumen, 2003), esp. 102–3.

44. Jacques Derrida, *Aporias*, trans. Thomas Dutoit (Stanford: Stanford University Press, 1993), 77.

45. Thanks to Martin Hägglund for this metaphor.

EPILOGUE

1. Ludwig Wittgenstein, *Philosophical Investigations*, trans. G. E. M. Anscombe (New York: Macmillan, 1953).

2. As Rorty says at the outset of his third volume of collected papers, almost no one says there is no such thing as truth, even if some philosophers are understood to be saying this. Richard Rorty, *Truth and Progress: Philosophical Papers, Volume 3* (Cambridge: Cambridge University Press, 1998).

3. See again Donald Davidson's classic intervention, "On the Very Idea of a Conceptual Scheme," *Proceedings and Addresses of the American Philosophical Association* 47 (1974).

4. Gilles Deleuze and Félix Guattari, *What Is Philosophy?* trans. Hugh Tomlinson and Graham Burchell (New York: Columbia University Press, 1994), 5.

5. Hans Ulrich Gumbrecht, *The Production of Presence: What Meaning Cannot Convey* (Stanford: Stanford University Press, 2004), xv.

6. Michel Foucault, *The History of Sexuality: Volume I: An Introduction,* trans. Robert Hurley (New York: Random House, 1990), 152.

7. Judith Butler, *Bodies That Matter* (New York: Routledge, 1993), chapter 1.

8. The work of Tim Dean strikes me as a particularly good example of this current. See, for example, *Beyond Sexuality* (Chicago: University of Chicago Press, 2000).

9. Jacques Derrida, *Resistances of Psychoanalysis*, trans. Peggy Kamuf et al. (Stanford: Stanford University Press, 1998), 27 (hereafter cited as *R*).

10. See, for example, Jacques Lacan, *Écrits: A Selection*, trans. Alan Sheridan (New York: W. W. Norton, 1977), 302.

11. Friedrich Nietzsche, *Nachgelassene Werke: Nietzsche's Werke*, Band XIV (Leipzig: Naumann, 1904), 369. See Joshua Landy's excellent discussion of what he calls "lucid self-delusion" in his book *Philosophy as Fiction: Self, Deception, and Knowledge in Proust* (Oxford: Oxford University Press, 2004).

Index

In this index an "f" indicates a separate reference on the next page; "ff" indicates separate references on the next two pages; "*passim*" indicates a cluster of references within a close but not consecutive sequence.